in_focus

Women
and Land

in_focus

IDRC's *in_focus* collection tackles current and pressing issues in sustainable international development. Each publication distills IDRC's research experience with an eye to drawing out important lessons, observations, and recommendations. Each also serves as a focal point for an IDRC website that probes more deeply into the issue and is constructed to serve the differing information needs of IDRC's various readers. A full list of in_focus websites may be found at **www.idrc.ca/in_focus**. Each *in_focus* book may be browsed and ordered online at **www.idrc.ca/books**.

IDRC welcomes any feedback on this publication. Please direct your comments to The Publisher at **info@idrc.ca**.

in_focus

Women
and Land

SECURING RIGHTS FOR BETTER LIVES

Debbie Budlender and Eileen Alma

INTERNATIONAL DEVELOPMENT RESEARCH CENTRE
Ottawa • Cairo • Dakar • Montevideo • Nairobi • New Delhi • Singapore

Published by the International Development Research Centre
PO Box 8500, Ottawa, ON, Canada K1G 3H9
www.idrc.ca / info@idrc.ca

© International Development Research Centre 2011

Library and Archives Canada Cataloguing in Publication

Budlender, Debbie
Women and land : securing rights for better lives / Debbie Budlender and
Eileen Alma.

(In focus)
Issued also in French under title : Les femmes et la terre, des droits fonciers
pour une meilleure vie.
Includes bibliographical references.
Available also on the Internet.
ISBN 978-1-55250-522-9

1. Sex discrimination against women--Developing countries.
2. Sex discrimination against women--Africa, Sub-Saharan.
3. Women landowners--Developing countries.
 4. Women landowners--Africa, Sub-Saharan.
5. Land tenure--Developing countries.
6. Land reform--Developing countries.
I. Alma, Eileen.
II. International Development Research Centre (Canada).
III. Title. IV. Series: In focus (International Development Research Centre
(Canada))

HQ1240.5 A4 B82 2011   305.4209172'4
C2011-980143-4
ISBN (e-book) 978-1-55250-525-0

This publication may be read online at **www.idrc.ca/books**, and serves as the
focal point for an IDRC thematic website on land rights, gender inequality,
and poverty: **www.idrc.ca/in_focus_womenandland.**

Contents

Part 3. Experiences from the field ➤ 25

With IDRC support, researchers, academics, grassroots activists, and community leaders throughout sub-Saharan Africa have worked together to explore the experiences of women from many angles: legal, customary, political, and economic.

Part 4. Lessons learned ➤ 67

The evidence presented in this book provides fresh insight for policymakers and others working to secure women's rights to land and thus strengthen the communities in which they live

5. Looking forward ➳ **73**

Much remains to be done, and IDRC continues to support research in this field. This final chapter points to some areas that are important to reflect on as we move forward.

Sources and resources ➳ **79**

Executive summary

The issue

Land is an important source of security against poverty across the developing world, but, in many places, unequal rights to land put women at a disadvantage, perpetuate poverty, and entrench gender inequality. Surprisingly little detailed information exists on women's relationship with land, and even less comes from women themselves. This book aims to help fill that gap, drawing on research funded by IDRC over many years.

The research

The core of this book focuses on recent findings from sub-Saharan Africa, where researchers in 14 countries have explored the topic from many angles: legal, customary, political, and economic. Researchers from non-governmental organizations (NGOs), academics, and grassroots activists worked together with communities, exploring the experiences of women in specific contexts. On the affiliated website, (**www.idrc.ca/in_focus_womenandland**), a series of five case studies is presented:

Land holds promise of peace in Colombia

With coloured pens and large sheets of white paper, a group of women in Colombia are bringing the past back to life. They map out the physical contours of the terrain they once called home and their experiences there. They draw their recollections of life before conflict. They draw the landmarks that were once part of their daily lives. They draw the events that forced them to leave.

This seemingly simple activity plays a potentially crucial role within Colombia's urgent quest to address one of its most pressing social problems. Unequal land distribution fed decades of bloody civil war and today continues to cast doubt on the viability of the country's uneasy peace.

Local solutions gain ground in East Africa

In the Mukono district of Uganda, a recently separated couple had a serious dispute over the family's land. The woman had taken out a loan to buy the land, and the husband had built a house on it. When the husband tried to sell the property after the separation, the woman appealed to a local court for the right to remain with the couple's three children on the family plot. The court was sympathetic. Arguing that the children's welfare was of primary concern, it ruled that the man could not sell the property and uproot his family.

In Uganda, Tanzania, and Kenya, a decentralized approach to land administration promises more accessible dispute resolution and a better deal for women. But the new systems face significant challenges. Among them are old social attitudes that pre-empt any real discussion about women's right to control land.

New attitudes key to progress in Malawi and Cameroon

At a recent funeral in Malawi, in a part of the country where customary law dictates that only men can own land, came a sign that old attitudes may slowly be changing. When the village chief rose to deliver his remarks, he shared with mourners some thoughts they likely did not expect to hear.

The chiefs act as custodians of customary law and are generally assumed to oppose statutory reforms that seek to extend new land rights to women. But on this day it was different. The chief spoke about the impact of traditional land-inheritance customs that routinely cast widowed or divorced women off the land they had worked with their husbands, rendering them unable to feed themselves or their children. This is an injustice against the wives, mothers, sisters, and daughters in our village, he said, and this should change.

Owning land a path out of poverty in Pakistan

In Pakistan, land ownership is recognized as the single most important factor keeping families out of poverty. Increasingly, more equal distribution of land is also acknowledged as key to halting environmental degradation and moving toward more sustainable forms of development. Poor, landless peasants are typically driven to overuse the few resources around them, fuelling a downward cycle of environmental destruction and deepening poverty. With the security that comes from owning land, those peasants have a greater incentive to preserve, rather than plunder, resources.

For decades, efforts to distribute agricultural land more equitably consistently excluded women. Then, a groundbreaking research project made women part of the discussion. It set the stage for a provincial campaign that for the first time in Pakistan's history transferred land to poor women.

Equality a collective effort in Senegal

Senegal is a country of many ethnicities and diverse agricultural zones. The Wolof and Sévère predominate in the country's Peanut

Basin, where they grow cash crops such as peanuts and millet. In the Casamance, most people are Diola and produce rice. In the wooded grasslands, Peul nomads use land to pasture livestock. People in these and other zones follow a variety of customs. No matter how diverse their practices may be, however, they share a common characteristic: they overlook women when making decisions about land.

Elected officials and religious leaders have joined forces with researchers documenting Senegalese women's unequal access to land. They are raising awareness among women, and men, while encouraging women to participate in decision-making bodies.

The lessons

Grounded in local realities, the evidence summarized in this book aims to capture the diversity and complexity of women's experiences. Most important, it provides fresh insights for policymakers and others working to secure women's rights to land and, thus, strengthen the communities in which they live. Here are a few of the most important lessons:

-► Participation-oriented research methods are much more likely to bring about immediate benefits than other, more traditional research methods.

-► Merely passing legislation is of little effect without the necessary resources for implementation, without informing and educating all relevant actors on the provisions of the legislation, without monitoring the reforms, and without effective sanctions on failure to implement.

-► It is crucial both to consult and involve women when designing reforms and monitoring their implementation.

➤ Women's access to land does not simply hinge on a choice
between customary and statutory systems. Rather, we are faced
with a more complex question of how the two systems interact
and are used by different groups of women and men. The
research also emphasizes the need to think about customary
law as "living" and evolving.

➤ Addressing land injustices requires varied approaches that
streamline and consolidate numerous land laws in a given
country. It is vital to establish and maintain links among
research, policy, practice, and people.

➤ The importance of providing teaching and training in a variety
of disciplines for a young generation of women in Africa
cannot be overstated.

Preface

THE ISSUE
On the web

Land is clearly a significant form of property in every part of the world and links the economic, cultural, political, and legal dimensions of social life. Land tenure systems that recognize the interests of all people are critical in advancing social and economic equity.

Yet discussions around land tenure often ignore issues of access and rights that are specific to women. In many countries, public policies have ignored differences between women's and men's property rights, and "the household" is often generalized — treated as a single unit with common interests where resources are pooled and shared.

For the past several years, Canada's International Development Research Centre (IDRC) has supported researchers gathering evidence that exposes and challenges gender discriminatory policies and practices related to land. This in_focus book is drawn almost entirely from the work of 24 IDRC-supported research teams in Africa. It also reflects those researchers' commitment to advancing women's rights and access to land by formulating concrete policy recommendations that can lead to social change.

IDRC is one of several organizations concerned with the critical socioeconomic and environmental issues that inevitably emerge from discussions of land tenure. A focus on women's land rights and land access has been a priority research stream for two IDRC programs: Rural Poverty and Environment and Women's Rights and Citizenship. The former program sought to strengthen the ability of the rural poor — particularly women, indigenous peoples, and ethnic minorities — to define and defend their rights to access such key resources as water, land, forests, fisheries, and rangelands. The Women's Rights and Citizenship program funded research geared toward realizing more quickly the objective — spelled out in the *Convention on the Elimination of All Forms of Discrimination against Women* (articles 14–16) and endorsed by the international community — that women should have equal access to land and other property (UN 1979). These two IDRC programs pooled resources and collaborated to fund much of the research that forms the basis of this book.

The geographic focus of the book is sub-Saharan Africa, where most of the research was conducted. Some 24 projects — varying in both size and methods — were conducted in 14 African countries. In September 2010, IDRC organized a symposium that brought 140 researchers to Nairobi, Kenya, to share the findings of their work among themselves and with a larger constituency that included grassroots women's organizations, national and local decision-makers, and the donor community (IDRC 2010). At the end of the symposium, participants contributed to a summary document of recommendations for policy and practice that reflects a shared vision for advancing women's rights agendas on the continent. Many of the extracts included in this book are from interviews conducted at this event.

We would like to acknowledge with deep thanks and appreciation the many researchers and colleagues (past and present) whose passion and work are the foundation of this book. Our special thanks go to Bob Stanley and Stephen Dale for their assistance with the editing of the book drafts and to members of the communications team at IDRC for their support and encouragement. We dedicate this book to African women, whether landowners, land-dwellers, workers, researchers, practitioners, or contributors to both family and the economy. They deserve our utmost respect as they seek to chart new pathways to claiming — or reclaiming — what is theirs by right.

Debbie Budlender is a specialist researcher with the Community Agency for Social Enquiry, a South African non-governmental social policy research organization.

Eileen Alma is a program officer at Canada's International Development Research Centre, where she focuses on the political, economic, and social rights of marginalized women.

On the web
THE ISSUE

Part 1

The issues and the development context

Development texts abound with general statements about women and poverty. These statements tend to categorize women as a "vulnerable group" needing special attention when, for example, poverty reduction strategies are implemented. Some of the statements focus on woman-headed households rather than women as individuals. They typically point to evidence that woman-headed households generally tend to be poorer than male-headed households (although this is not the case in all countries).

Many general statements also emphasize the fact that particular groups of women — typically rural women and widows — are most likely to be poor. Some point out that rural people tend to be poorer than urban people, and that women — because they are more likely than men to be living in rural areas — are at a particular disadvantage.

Women's confinement to poor rural areas is partly related to the fact that men are more likely to migrate to urban areas for work and other purposes. In the Manhiça district of Mozambique, for example, large numbers of men travel to South Africa to work in the mines or to Maputo, the capital, to find other work. As our Mozambican research team notes, this means the women who stay at home become the heads of their families and assume control of the local rural economy (Andrade et al. 2009). Despite these responsibilities, however, they remain dependent on men to control and register the land.

Women and land

Linked to women's predominance in rural areas is the greater likelihood that they will be dependent on land for their livelihoods, as well as for a place to live and raise their families. In many parts of Africa, the majority of the population is still rural, and the overwhelming majority of rural households do agricultural work. About 73% of Tanzania's people, for example, live in rural areas and depend on subsistence agriculture (Kassim 2011).

Although the agriculture-related tasks of women, men, and children usually differ, women often put in the most hours. That is *before* taking into account the many other unpaid care tasks that they do, including housework, cooking, and caring for children and sick or elderly household members. Furthermore, women are far more likely than men to be classified — both by themselves and by the men in their household — as unpaid "family helpers."

Given this general understanding that women are more concentrated in rural areas, more dependent on land, and more likely to be poor, it is clear that land is a central issue and is key to advancing the rights and well-being of women in Africa. This has long been recognized. The informal slogan of the United Nations' Decade for Women (1975–85), for example, stated that "while women do two-thirds of the world's work, they receive 10 percent of the world's income and own 1 percent of the means of production."

Although that slogan focuses on women's low rate of land ownership as the crux of the issue, gender theorists have recently been looking at the relation between women and land in more complex terms, considering the distinctions between access to, use of, and control over land. The source and accuracy of the figures quoted above are unknown, but it is worth noting that, unless we know the percentage of the means of production owned by men, the 1% is questionable. It could be that a large percentage of land — especially in Africa — is owned neither by individual men nor women, but instead communally or by the state.

Access, use, and control

Rural sociologists Jesse Ribot and Nancy Lee Peluso's (2003) definition of access as "the ability to derive benefits from things including material objects, persons, institutions, and symbols," leads them to conceive of access as "a bundle of powers" rather than necessarily a "bundle of rights." The distinction among access, use, and control is particularly important given the prevalence in Africa of customary land tenure systems, which often contain no equivalent to the Western concept of "ownership." This distinction is much more than just an exercise in semantics. Although many poor rural women have access to land and use it, they are generally far less likely than men to have control over it and its products or to own it. In practical terms, as many of the research projects referred to later in this book will show, this lack

> Interventions aimed simply at giving women access
> to the land on which they work will not necessarily
> enhance their well-being or afford them control
> over their lives.

of control places many women in highly insecure and precarious situations. Many women who have only conditional access to land may lose it when their husbands die; others may lose the right to use the land their livelihoods depend on if male family or community members believe they can profit by selling it. This is an especially significant threat to women in an era of rising land prices, increasing land scarcity, and rising competition to control this resource.

Given these sorts of common occurrences, the Makerere Institute for Social Research (2010), which oversaw the IDRC-sponsored research in Kenya, Uganda, and Rwanda, concludes that "the general consensus in all the three countries is that women's access to land is not an issue; the problem is lack of control and ownership."

The distinction among access, use, and control of land also has important implications for policymaking. Examining the specific types of relations that women have to land reveals the ways in which they are vulnerable. This, in turn, leads to a realization that interventions aimed simply at giving women access to the land on which they work will not necessarily enhance their well-being or afford them control over their lives.

However, although women face the challenges described above in general terms, gendered power relations over land and resources are continually being negotiated, contested, and resisted in various ways. This book aims to contribute to the ability of women and those who see themselves as their supporters to engage in such struggles.

We recognize that, unless we look at particular situations faced by particular groups of women in particular locations, it is difficult to craft policies that assist women seeking greater control over their lives. Beyond our general understanding of the importance of land and policy for women, we need to examine how specific factors, such as marital status, types of marriage, age, class, and variations in cultural contexts, create special challenges for women in particular situations.

The researchers whose work is presented in this book have taken such an approach. Their focus on understanding the "differences" that define women's particular experiences reflects a growing realization that embracing complexity is key to understanding and achieving real and tangible change.

Land tenure and customary law

The gender and land tenure debate is complicated by the intricacies of diverse land tenure regimes. These may encompass complex informal and formal systems based on religion or custom, as well as on legal and governing frameworks. Research in many countries makes it clear that land tenure regimes often consist of overlapping legal spheres that bring together different norms, rules, and sanctions in various combinations. It is against this backdrop that gender-based land tenure struggles take place.

Customary laws and practices are an explicit focus of several of the research projects supported by IDRC, including large-scale surveys conducted in Cameroon and South Africa. Even where this is not an explicit focus, most of the projects discuss custom to some extent, revealing its centrality even in countries where legislation has attempted to downplay its influence. The key roles played by "traditional" leaders are also evident from several of the projects. In Zimbabwe, for example, the headman still has a role in land redistribution in that country's Fast Track Land Reform Programme

(Mazhawidza and Manjengwa 2011), implying that the possibility of reducing gender inequalities through reform programs is complicated by customary practice.

At least two issues relate directly to customary law and practice. The first concerns the interplay between customary laws and systems and "Western" or statutory laws. What the laws (including constitutions) say and what happens in practice are not necessarily the same. The second issue relates to how customary law affects access to (and control over) land and security of tenure. Here the focus includes reforms relating to registration of land ownership as well as reforms relating to marriage.

Decentralization

In most African countries, there have been reforms leading to greater decentralization of service delivery and governance (Table 1). Decentralization here refers to the transfer of functions, resources, and varying degrees of political and fiscal autonomy to regional, local, or municipal governments. In relation to land, the reforms often involve the establishment of institutions responsible for land registration, resolution of disputes, and the like. Thus decentralization can provide new opportunities for women and men to participate in, and be represented in, matters that closely affect their lives.

However, approaches to decentralization differ in extent, in the seriousness with which they are undertaken, and in the resources allocated to their implementation, among other factors. Further, although potentially offering opportunities for women in terms of participation, decentralization can also have a negative impact on women's access to and control over land.

Some of the reforms explicitly include gender aspects. For example, several countries specify quotas for women in the new institutions. However, the IDRC-funded research projects suggest

Table 1.	Examples of reforms featuring decentralization of land administration in East Africa.

Country	Reform
Tanzania	• Undergoing a Local Government Reform Programme to facilitate decentralization and increase citizen participation in governance at a local level.
	• Ministry of Regional Administration and Local Government created in 1998 to oversee implementation.
	• Objective of decentralization is to deliver services according to locally defined needs comprising good governance, accountability and transparency, and autonomy, including citizen participation in decision-making.
Kenya	• The Kenyan constitution, passed in 2010, provides for a two-tier devolution system: national and county governments.
	• A key goal for the county governments is to give self-governance power to the people and enhance participation in the development process. Unlike other forms of decentralization that Kenya has tried, devolved county governments are constitutionally mandated to have some legislative powers and form their own governments. Each of 47 counties will be headed by a governor. No more than two-thirds of the members of a county government representative body shall be the same gender.
Uganda	• The *Land Act* (Uganda 1998) operationalizes the principles laid down in the country's constitution (Uganda 1995), providing for tenure, ownership, and management of land; consolidating the law relating to tenure, ownership, and management of land; and providing for other related or incidental matters.
	• The Land Sector Strategic Plan 2001–2011 (Uganda 2010) is the framework for implementing sector-wide reforms and land management including the *Land Act*. The plan facilitates the decentralization of land services and the devolution of land management.
	• The *Land (Amendment) Act, 2004* (Uganda 2004) reduced the number of prescribed land administration institutions from land committees at the parish level to the subcounty and scrapped subcounty and village land boards. It also increased the bargaining power of tenants by controlling ground rents and protecting them from eviction.

On the web
THE ISSUE

that the reforms and new "rules" are often poorly communicated and not widely known even among those directly responsible for their implementation. Even when they are known, a range of social (including gender), economic, and other forces often affect how — and even whether — they are implemented. Several of the research projects focused on decentralization, whereas, in others, decentralization emerged as an issue in the course of the research.

Land policies and reforms

New land policies and reforms sometimes include elements that attempt to address gender issues explicitly, for example, gender equality clauses. Some land policies do not include such clauses, but nevertheless have different impacts on women and men and on different subgroups of women and men. In particular, policies that attempt to commercialize and privatize land, in the hope that this will promote investment and economic growth, can have negative consequences on women's access to and control over land.

Economic dimensions

Because land is a key "means of production," any discussion of women and land must consider the economic dimensions. This is not to deny the symbolic value of land. Indeed, as several of the research projects emphasize, land is central to citizenship because a nation is defined in terms of territory. Further, in many African belief systems, land represents an important link to ancestors. Providing space for burials is one of the ways that land serves this spiritual function.

That said, the economic dimensions are key for many rural people because land represents a route to survival and food security as well as — if one is optimistic — economic empowerment. Land tenure policy and practice play a key role in determining whether wealth and land ownership will remain highly concentrated or whether it becomes possible to achieve — through redistribution programs — greater social equality and gender parity. Land tenure policies are also often critical in determining what types of crops are grown and whether land users feel secure enough to employ sustainable practices and not overexploit the land.

"Economic" is often seen narrowly, in terms of money, income earning, and self-sufficiency. Feminist economists have questioned this narrow interpretation in relation to the unpaid provision of multiple services — housework, cooking, caring for others — carried out daily by most women in their homes. Such unpaid care is recognized as "work" and "production" by the United Nations and by bodies such as the World Bank and the Organisation for Economic Co-operation and Development. Nevertheless, it is not always "counted" when calculating gross domestic product and, thus, is not "seen" by many economists, even though it is key to the development of human resources and the general well-being of families and individuals.

> People's understanding of land is based not on existing formal legal categories but on the utility of land in their everyday lives.

Extending the concept of the economic in relation to land opens one's eyes to land's primary importance as a place to reside safely and securely. Research in Cameroon (Fonjong et al. 2009) exposed a gender difference in the extent to which ordinary women and men (never mind economists) recognize this element. The research revealed that people's understanding of land is based not on existing formal legal categories but on the utility of land in their everyday lives.

According to the Cameroon study, most women view land primarily as a source of livelihood and food. Its value as a factor of production is secondary. Men, on the other hand, regard land primarily as a factor of production, secondarily as a source of wealth and status, next as a source of livelihood and food, and finally as habitat. Clearly, women and men have different interests with respect to ownership and control of land.

Some statistics on use of land from the research projects suggest that it would be misguided for land policies to assume that all rural people see land primarily as an agricultural production asset. In a survey of 108 women conducted by Kenya's Young Widows Advancement Program (2011), 20% lived on the land but did not use it for agriculture or other income-earning purposes. In contrast, in Rwanda, 10 of the 50 women involved in land disputes did not live on the disputed land; however, in 41 of those cases, the main use of the land under dispute was agriculture. In South Africa, a little more than a quarter of the women interviewed lived in homesteads that had access to fields. Fewer than half of the homesteads with fields had used them in the past 12 months.

It is perhaps not surprising that women, in particular, recognize the importance of land beyond its use for agricultural production. Their attitude results in large part from the public–private divide, as women are likely to spend more of their lives in the private space of the "home" or even, in some cases, be confined there. They have responsibility for children and families, which restricts their mobility. Given these roles, women can be expected to be especially concerned about security of tenure.

The impact of HIV/AIDS

The devastating effects of the HIV/AIDS epidemic in Africa have also given prominence to the question of security of tenure for women. In many African cultures, access to land for married women occurs through their husbands. Thus, the increasing likelihood that husbands will die at a young age increases the number of women whose tenure is insecure and who, therefore, face the prospect of not having a place to live. In some cultures, a widow retains the right to live in the husband's homestead through a system under which she is forced to have sex with, or even marry, one of her late husband's male relatives. In a situation of high HIV-prevalence, this is not an attractive option for either party, and incidents of women losing access have thus increased.

Women's loss of land on widowhood was a key concern in two research projects in Kenya. However, security of tenure is not confined to situations of high HIV/AIDS prevalence. It can also be an issue at times of political conflict, land invasions, and other upheavals. This issue is discussed in more detail in Part 3.

Natural resource management

Land rights are only one measure of the security of women's livelihoods. There is also the issue of productive resources, such as water and forests, that are governed by various sets of frameworks, norms, and values involving complex social relations. Such linked resources are frequently affected by social structures and customs that can impede women's rights to land use.

It is widely acknowledged that, despite women's complex relationship with productive resources, they tend to remain outside the associated decision-making processes, for cultural or other reasons. For instance, although women are most affected by access to potable water, they often remain on the periphery of local water management institutions, such as water users' associations. Women may own land for agricultural production, but institutional impediments often make it difficult for them to obtain irrigation rights.

> In patriarchal systems, men tend to control the
> resources, such as land and associated irrigation
> rights, even though women are the primary users.

Communal resources are essential to the livelihood strategies of
many in rural communities, particularly marginalized groups or
individuals who are unable to access individual resource rights.
Use of common property typically includes access to resources,
such as wetlands and fuel harvesting.

Beyond land policy

The research described in this book was conducted against a background of past and ongoing reforms. Many of these reforms relate
to land in general, and some — such as the formalization of legal
systems — have gender equality among their objectives. Some also
address gender-related issues directly. Many other reforms, such as
decentralization or commercialization, are not necessarily seen as
addressing gender issues or affecting gender relations, but have
marked gendered impacts, both positive and negative. However, as
Razavi (2003) observed, the introduction of "modern" forms of
property titling has often strengthened men's lands claims while
women's customary claims to land have been weakened.

Investigating the impact of reforms was one of the aims of many
of the research projects. Some sought to determine to what
extent reforms, which were expected to promote gender equality,
had succeeded and, when this did not happen, why they failed.

> There is a growing consensus that solutions to women's land
> tenure problems need to be grounded in local specificities...
> However, in policy terms, this presents practical challenges...
> there have been remarkable similarities in diagnoses and policy
> prescriptions regarding women's land tenure interests across
> Africa in spite of agreements about the need for policies to take
> differences among women into account. Tsikata (2010)

In some cases, the research looked at the success or failure of other reforms, not directly concerned with land, that attempted to address gender equality and the ways in which these reforms have affected access to and control over land. The Rwanda case study, for example, focuses on legislation with respect to marriage, which, in turn, should influence women's rights to land.

Some of the findings from the research will be useful in the development of policies and interventions in such areas as climate change, the environment, and food security. The Mozambique research, with its focus on cultivation of the biofuel jatropha, is a key example. As explained in one of the Mozambique research documents, although promotion of jatropha production has worthy environmental objectives, to date, it has had negative impacts on some women. The research focused on Manhiça, one of the districts targeted in negotiations between the Government of Mozambique and foreign investors. The researchers' objective was to see whether and how women managed to get grants for land in a context in which the land for subsistence agriculture has been gradually shifted to commercial agriculture, especially biofuel production.

> *Jatropha is one of the plants which are used to produce biofuels.... But, in fact, even this being a positive intention, it becomes at the end of the day something that is hurting, is being harmful to communities.... At this time you see the issue of jatropha. But at the site of the cane plantation for supplying the sugar industry you find another aspect, which is that other natural resources like water is being shifted from benefiting the communities or the local farmers to be supplying the sugar industry.* Graça Samo, Forum Mulher (2009)

In Part 2 we review the approach taken by IDRC to identify and address these issues in parts of Africa. Part 3 describes the findings of many of these diverse projects funded by the Centre.

Part 2

The approach

Identifying critical areas for research

IDRC-supported research on women's rights and access to land began early in the new millennium with a project on gender, globalization, and land tenure that aimed to understand gender and natural resource management. The project supported research in Ghana, Cameroon, and Kenya that examined how macro-level relations around land tenure are linked to those at the micro-level. The case studies subsequently extended to Vietnam, Brazil, Bolivia, and Peru and became the basis for *Land Tenure, Gender, and Globalization,* co-published by IDRC and Zubaan (Tsikata and Golah 2010).

IDRC built on this initial project by prioritizing research on women's rights and access to land in sub-Saharan Africa, working with research institutions in both single- and multi-country studies. The program's approach was based on contemporary feminist scholarship, which contends that if women are to be empowered to claim their citizenship rights, then economic independence and security of livelihoods must be addressed in tandem with political and social empowerment.

A series of in-depth studies was commissioned to provide the basis for a program of support to improve the situation of rural women. Although these subregional studies pointed to common issues and potential solutions across geographic boundaries, they also helped highlight specific local realities that make individual contexts and situations unique. Each study was designed to:

- ➤ Identify key organizations, networks, and individuals active in gender and land tenure issues
- ➤ Provide a concise synopsis of work done by organizations engaged in research and development
- ➤ Identify critical issues that need to be addressed.

In addition, the studies identified opportunities for research that could add value to existing work and address means to improving women's access and rights to land and resources. The studies involved regional literature reviews, consultations with numerous organizations engaged in gender and tenure issues in selected countries, and, in some cases, field visits to related projects. This book focuses on the issues raised in these studies that recur as themes across many projects. The exploration of these themes in part 3 highlights similarities where these clearly exist.

The need for evidence beyond generalities

As we noted in Part 1, a chief objective of the IDRC-sponsored research was to deepen understanding of how rural women's limited land rights make them more susceptible to poverty. The researchers aimed to move beyond the generalities that support this position by compiling detailed evidence showing how a range of factors (e.g., marriage and types of marriage, the roles of men and children, class, race, and cultural distinctions) play out for particular women in particular communities.

As the University of Nairobi's Patricia Kameri-Mbote remarks, this type of research, exploring the impacts of specific conditions on specific groups of women, was previously in short supply:

The dominant narratives... [have been] on women, not on women in these particular communities. So it's almost like these women fall between different discussions, where you have discussions about women and then discussions about communities, but no discussion about women in those communities.
Patricia Kameri-Mbote, University of Nairobi

An advantage of research that captures the experience of a broad range of women within their own communities is that it is more likely to point toward policy solutions that will be of benefit to more than just one group. (For example, if older widows are taken as representative of all women, the subsequent policies built around that assumption are likely to exclude women who don't fit the profile.) Policies that address a multitude of factors will almost assuredly be useful in more places, for more women. In addition, they are more likely to address the root causes that sustain — in a variety of ways depending on the particular setting — women's social and economic inequality. Policies based on generalities, by contrast, are more vulnerable to being irrelevant to many of the women they are ostensibly designed to help.

The scope and range of the research referred to in this book reflects this understanding of the importance of place and local differences. We draw primarily on 24 IDRC-supported research projects carried out in 14 African countries. The decision to focus on Africa stems from a recognition that previous conclusions about women and land drawn from studies in Asia may not apply on this continent. Nor may findings from one part of Africa necessarily be applicable in another, given the immense diversity that exists across and even within African countries. Drawing from research undertaken in a number of African countries, therefore, allows us to account for this diversity and note the similarities and differences that exist in different settings.

On the web
THE RESEARCH

Evidence generated by whom?

IDRC's decision to fund particular types of research on women's rights and access to land grew out of a concern that it is rarely the affected women themselves who talk and write about their issues. A related concern was that the affected women are rarely involved, or even consulted, when policies to address "their problems" are drawn up. Many of the research projects thus placed particular emphasis on hearing the voices of rural women. Some focused specifically on women who had attempted to claim their land-related rights. Further, the research teams often included, or collaborated with, organizations working with rural women.

In this manner, rural women became not simply research subjects, but also partners and agents for change. Nor did the research focus only on hearing rural women's voices: critical challenges face women in urban settings, and the urban–rural dividing lines are often blurred by migration. Thus, in a few cases the research also involved women in urban settings.

The research was undertaken by individuals in a wide range of institutions and included several partnerships. Teams at well-known research centres in African universities conducted critical research — both theoretical and policy-oriented. In addition, several projects were undertaken with NGOs (sometimes working in collaboration with academic centres) or government bodies. Research teams included specialists in social, economic, legal, and environmental issues.

IDRC's research-grant-awarding processes typically place significant emphasis on strengthening capacities. Most, if not all, projects on gender and land rights included some level of capacity building. At the organizational level, methodological training in data collection and analysis was provided; at the individual level, capacity building included funding for a new generation of women scholars, either as research assistants or as collaborating doctoral students. In addition, IDRC and grant recipients engaged

Unusual research collaborators

The variety of institutions involved in the Madagascar action-research project illustrates the way in which some of the IDRC projects promoted collaboration between partners who might not ordinarily work together. The Madagascar project is especially interesting in that a government agency took the lead. The partnership included:

- Centre National pour le Développement Rural, a national government research centre that works on agriculture and gender issues, as the lead agency
- Solidarité des Intervenants sur le Foncier, a non-governmental national umbrella association working on land issues
- FilazanaVaovaoTsy Marina, a non-governmental federation of rural women's associations
- Réseau Syndical des Organisations Agricoles, a national umbrella organization of farmers' associations
- Harmonisation des Actions pour la Réalisation d'un Développement Intégré, an NGO working on development issues including land and tenure security

The intent of this design was to encourage greater engagement by the community at large with land issues in the country, thereby heightening awareness of women's land issues. This was expected to improve gender-sensitive analysis and planning and increase the potential for policy change. Adopting this model also provided an opportunity to build knowledge about the importance of research and to build capacity around research design. The end result for the Madagascar collaboration, as well as others, was greater local ownership of the research.

On the web **THE RESEARCH**

in direct capacity-building efforts by bringing together cohorts of research teams for training in communications and dissemination techniques. In the final analysis, one of the most important outcomes of this research was an increased capacity for gender analysis regarding an issue that is of critical importance for Africa.

Global collaboration

From the outset, it was important to engage other major global actors for whom questions of land tenure and administration are of primary concern. Thus, IDRC developed strategic partnerships for some of the programming at the beginning of the research planning cycle. For example, project planning on gender and land included the establishment of a global advisory group comprising representatives of the United Nations' Food and Agriculture Organization, the International Land Coalition (ILC), the International Fund for Agricultural Development, the International Food Policy Research Institute, the International Center for Research on Women, the Canadian International Development Agency, and the International Institute for Environment and Development.

This advisory group, along with experts from several African regions, met in May 2006 to map a way forward. Participants agreed that the central question for researchers seeking to contribute to a transformative agenda was, "How can the research empower women and encourage agency?" They also agreed that it was crucial to synthesize and complement existing information, rather than just produce new research.

IDRC also built relations with prominent organizations toward the end of the research cycle, to enhance dissemination and outreach and to build the support that could lead to increased policy influence. Building on its recent successful experiences in partnerships around decentralization, local rights, and women's empowerment, IDRC worked with the United Nations Development Programme, UN-HABITAT, and several bilateral donor agencies to showcase and share the work of research partners across the African continent. IDRC also built relations with grassroots women leaders through the Huairou Commission. This is a global coalition that attempts to enhance grassroots women's organizations' community development practices and enable them, collectively, to exercise political power at the global level.

Research methods

One of the challenges of consolidating a large body of research is to reconcile different research approaches. The research highlighted in this book is often classified as either "action" research or "comparative" research. Each approach has its own merits and offers its own challenges.

More than half the projects employed action research, which is driven by stakeholder participation and can strengthen actions and capacity at the local level. For example, capacity building in data collection can be linked to grassroots activism through the collection of stories and by bringing women and their organizations together to exchange their experiences. Action research – especially when it involves recording or documenting and sharing information – builds capacity to acquire sound qualitative data and, thereby, contributes to a process of empowerment. The downside is that action research sometimes raises expectations that research teams are not capable of fulfilling.

Other projects employed a comparative research approach, which focuses on extracting common themes and lessons across districts, countries, and subregions. For example, some involved comparative cross-country examination of decentralized land systems and the changes they are undergoing. When undertaken in partnership with key organizations and actors committed to moving an agenda forward, this approach can enhance collaboration among those groups. Comparative research requires a common theoretical and methodological framework, which means the projects must have at least some research questions in common.

Managing community partnerships

The research project undertaken by Kenya's Young Windows Advancement Program illustrates how it is possible to handle sensitively the tensions that can arise when different objectives and methods are used in research and organization. In this project, 108 widows residing in Kayole were interviewed using structured questionnaires. The researchers then used the information to select women who would participate in subsequent action research, which included unstructured home-based interviews that took close to a full day. Bimonthly group meetings were held with the wider group to discuss why these women had been selected. In this way, the researchers attempted to ensure that those not selected would not feel resentment. For the action research sessions, interviewers took along a food basket for the family in acknowledgement of the time burden posed by the interview and in line with the African culture of hospitality. This underscores the importance of knowing and being sensitive to community needs and concerns; this approach helped build community trust, ensuring in turn that researchers were able to gather reliable data.

Similarly, it was important to the Uganda Rural Development and Training Programme to cultivate a deep understanding of the communities under study. Researchers were able to discover that their research sample had become biased, because they were sufficiently tuned into community dynamics to notice that their contact people in the village were recommending only interviewees who shared their own social characteristics. (In this case, the process was leading to over-representation of married women.) The contact people were also selecting friends and relatives in the hope that they might gain financially by participating.

Many researchers emphasized the importance of working with other stakeholders in the community, rather than just with women. Some noted, for instance, that the role of men should be addressed, as a failure to do so might lead to resentment or even violence in contexts where new opportunities are opened for women but not for men. In areas where customary law is predominant, some felt it important to engage with traditional leaders who were likely to pass judgement on the action research projects based on their own understanding of the customary laws. Involving courts, police, and other institutional actors may also be useful when addressing the gap between policy or legal frameworks and implementation.

Competitive grants program

About a third of the projects were overseen by the ILC as a major action-oriented research program with a competitive small-grants model for project selection. The program was managed by the Makerere Institute for Social Research (Uganda) in East Africa and the Institute for Poverty, Land and Agrarian Studies (South Africa) in Southern Africa. Ten action-research projects were supported, and all are represented in this book.

On the web THE RESEARCH

In addition to research support, the ILC also undertook innovative elements regarding capacity building and advocacy. For example, the Advocacy Toolbox explains the importance of advocacy for development work, details what is required of an advocacy worker, and provides pointers on how to undertake strategic planning to present issues effectively (Lebert and Lebert 2010). The ILC contracted the Procasur Research Institute (2010) to help develop a "learning route" for 24 stakeholders involved in the competitive grants. A learning route is an innovative approach in which a variety of stakeholders are brought to communities that have faced development challenges. In this case, the primary objective of the visits was to identify a range of strategies to secure women's land rights. The visits helped educate researchers about the daily realities of the women they were studying, which ultimately led them to consider how their research findings could be more effectively translated into meaningful policy recommendations and changes in practice.

In Part 3 of this book we offer a selection of the findings from the research projects, complemented by profiles and case studies of women and land as well as a set of recommendations for policy and practice.

Part 3

Experiences from the field

This chapter presents findings and experiences from the IDRC-funded research projects undertaken in select locations in East and Southern Africa and, to a lesser extent, in Central and West Africa. The success of these locally based projects in highlighting traits and circumstances that are common to the various research sites — as well as the multitude of distinctions that separate them — suggests that this comparative approach has indeed helped deepen and broaden our understanding of issues surrounding women's land rights and access. Research on this topic in other countries, for example, countries in North Africa, may complement the findings presented here.

Beyond being strongly locally oriented, the research focused mainly on rural areas, reflecting the fact that the largest proportion of the population of African countries remains rural and that especially large proportions of women live and work in rural areas. Nevertheless, this focus should not be understood to mean that land problems — particularly gendered problems related to land — disappear when people live in urban areas.

The strong links that often exist between urban and rural areas in relation to land issues is illustrated by research conducted by the Young Widows Advancement Program in Kenya, a community-based self-help organization. The program was launched informally a decade ago by five young widows whose husbands had died from AIDS and who had been chased away from their matrimonial homes as a result. All five women tested HIV positive. Because of the stigma attached to HIV and AIDS, they met secretly to support each other by sharing experiences and organizing a rotating savings and credit organization that would provide money to purchase household items or start a business. The group operates from a rescue centre for young widows and orphans in Kayole Estate, a poor area of Nairobi that is home to many young women who lost their matrimonial homes following the death of their husbands.

Many of the young widows lost rural property because their late husbands had migrated to Nairobi. Although some husbands had invested in the rural ancestral land, that did not prevent the women from being evicted. Some of these women have little or no connection to their husband's rural land, which exacerbates the challenge of claiming land rights as widows. Other widows have moved to Nairobi for the first time after the death of their husbands. These young women often end up as petty traders or doing domestic or other casual, low-paid work.

Esther Angudha of the Young Widows Advancement Program says the widows would prefer to live in a rural area because of the women's spiritual connection with the land and also because urban life can be demeaning:

> Why the rural land or the agricultural land? The rural land has better rights.... So instead of waiting until you die, then there is a dilemma — where are you going to be buried? It is better to get your family land so that you are buried there. Plus you can also stop living as a squatter in town, because the jobs they were doing here is hawking, doing petty trade, and turning to prostitution.

The research carried out by Grassroots Organizations Operating Together in Sisterhood (GROOTS) in Kenya also has an urban link. GROOTS conducted interviews with dispossessed widows in the Gatundu district, a peri-urban area two hours' drive from Nairobi. GROOTS' research report (GROOTS 2011) notes that this proximity to the city and the relative ease of rural–urban migration for young people in search of better opportunities has contributed to the increased prevalence of HIV in Gatundu.

Aspects of diversity

The major challenges and priorities for women confronting land access issues vary greatly from country to country, in part because of differences in political and legal histories and structures. The Makerere Institute of Social Research's synthesis report (2010) on research in Kenya, Uganda, and Rwanda, for example, notes that the situations researchers found in each of those places required different solutions. Kenyan researchers felt that a major issue was the contradiction between customary and statutory laws and the resultant opportunities for "forum shopping" in the case of a dispute. In Uganda, which has a longer history of gender mainstreaming by government, the researchers were concerned about lack of implementation of laws that were intended to promote gender equality. In Rwanda, researchers felt that the government's ongoing reconstruction and reform process presented an opportunity for influencing developments.

On the web

THE RESEARCH

The degree of institutional capacity in particular countries may also determine the degree and type of challenges that rural women face. As researcher Patricia Kameri-Mbote expressed it while in Tanzania,

> [Tanzanians] are a little bit more orderly because there is the Village Land Act [and] they... have very well organized local level institutions for managing land.... In Uganda... [it is] probably a lot more erratic because they don't have as long a history of titling land.

Even within a seemingly homogenous group at a specific location, members may have a diversity of needs. The Young Widows Advancement Program, for example, found that among the group of widows in Kenya, the growing number of young women widowed because of the AIDS pandemic face different problems than older women. For example, a young widow cannot rely on support from adult sons as older widows generally can. In addition, a young widow's in-laws might argue against granting her ownership of property on the grounds that she is likely to remarry.

There are other problems too. Some chiefs reported being accused of having "inappropriate relationships" with young widows when they supported their claims to their deceased husbands' land and other property. As one chief explained, "Sometimes I have to involve the regular police in order to avoid scandal."

Variation in culture and customs between geographic areas was another factor that researchers had to account for. For example, the South African research project involved a large survey conducted in three different areas with different languages and cultures. Within each area, the randomly selected survey respondents included women from all marital status categories. In designing the project and analyzing results, the researchers paid particular attention to the different situations and experiences between and across groups.

The Malawi project examined differences between the experiences of women in patrilineal and matrilineal societies. The Madagascar research explicitly pointed out that most of the women interviewed during fieldwork were married and that the findings should, thus, not be extrapolated beyond this group. The Madagascar research also usefully highlighted the differences in the experiences of women from more and less wealthy backgrounds.

Women in the rich family have more control of the land. Why? Because, although she moves into the husband's village, the family — the couple — can buy land. So, since the land belongs to the couple, therefore, the lady, the woman, has more rights on this land. But for the women belonging to the poor or the medium family, they have far less control on the land. Of course, those women have access to land but they have, we can say, no control over this land. Danièle Ramiaramanana, Centre National de la Recherche Appliquée au Développement Rural

The relationship between customary and statutory law

Customary law or customary practices are mentioned in virtually all the research projects, even when this is not the explicit topic of the research. This highlights the extent to which custom continues to play a role in the lives of rural women and men even where formal laws seem to restrict its powers.

The "official" relation between customary and statutory law differs from one country to another. In several, it is common for statutory laws to recognize customary laws and practices in situations where such laws and practices do not contradict human rights, including women's rights. Such clauses are found in legislation ranging from national constitutions to specific laws and are in line with Article 17 of the *Universal Declaration of Human Rights*, which states that: "Everyone has the right to own property alone, as well as in association with others. No one shall arbitrarily be deprived of property" (UN 1948).

Such clauses are also in line with Article 16 of the *Convention on Elimination of All Forms of Discrimination against Women*, which declares that state parties must take measures to eliminate discrimination and ensure equal rights for spouses in respect of ownership, acquisition, management, administration, enjoyment, and disposition of property (UN 1979).

In Uganda, the Constitution (Uganda 1995) and the *Land Act 1998* (Uganda 1998) were the first laws to give formal recognition to customary land tenure, which had previously been beyond the realm of the law. Article 237(4)(a) of the Constitution and section 5(1) of the *Land Act* also provide for the registration of customary land rights, requiring all Ugandan citizens owning land under customary tenure to acquire certificates of ownership. Articles 237(5) and (6) further provide for the conversion of both customary and leasehold land tenures to freehold.

The challenge associated with provisions that formalize customary rights is that, in many customary systems, men are privileged with respect to access and control and what could be considered the equivalent of ownership. Thus, ironically, the normalization of customary rights can weaken any rights that women have under customary systems. Section 28 of Uganda's *Land Act* can be seen as an attempt to address this danger. It states:

> *Any decision taken in respect of land held under customary tenure, whether in respect of land held individually or communally, shall be in accordance with the custom, traditions and practices of the community, concerned; except that a decision which denies women or children or persons with disability access to ownership, occupation or use of any land imposes conditions which violate articles 33, 34 and 35 of the Constitution on any ownership, occupation or use of any land shall be null and void.* (Uganda 1998)

Section 40(1) extends protection beyond the time when land rights are formalized by requiring a spouse's consent to any transfer of household land. As discussed below, the spousal consent clause was the focus of one of the IDRC-funded research projects.

In other countries, protection of women's rights is also built into land laws. For example, Tanzania's *Village Land Act*, 1999 recognizes existing customary land rights but stipulates that those that deny women and other vulnerable groups lawful access to "ownership, occupation and use of land" would be considered violations of the principles of natural justice (Tanzania 1999).

It is especially important for statutory law to address inheritance, as customary law often provides only for male inheritance. In some cases, inheritance follows the principle of primogeniture, i.e., inheritance only by the eldest son. (This assumes, of course, that there are sons.)

Section 82 of the Kenyan Constitution allows customary laws to be applied to matters of succession (Kenya 2010). Customary laws of succession are also explicitly recognized in several other Kenyan laws, such as the *Africans' Wills Act* (Cap. 169) and the *Registered Land Act* (Kenya 2009).

However, the *Judicature Act* (Kenya 2007, article 3[2]) provides that:

> The High Court, the Court of Appeal and all subordinate courts shall be guided by African customary law in civil cases in which one or more of the parties is subject to it or affected by it, so far as it is applicable and is not repugnant to justice and morality or inconsistent with any written law, and shall decide all such cases according to substantial justice without undue regard to technicalities of procedure and without undue delay.

Kenya's National Land Policy of 2009 protects the rights of women and provides for joint spousal registration of land and spousal consent when land is sold, inheritance rights for unmarried daughters, and proportionate representation of women in institutions dealing with land.

THE RESEARCH
On the web

The laws are there and, strangely, the statutory laws within Kenya support property inheritance rights of widows, but at the same time it allows for customary and religious laws to operate. And most people take advantage of this to employ the customary law. Esther Angudha, Young Widows Advancement Program

Defining customary law and practice

The constitutions of both Mozambique and South Africa recognize customary norms as long as they do not undermine constitutional principles. For example, South Africa's *Bill of Rights*, which is embedded in the Constitution (South Africa 1996), states clearly that there must be no discrimination on the basis of race, gender, or other differences between people. Section 211(1) of the Constitution recognizes the "institution, status and role of traditional leadership, according to Customary law," but states that customary law is subject to the Constitution, including the *Bill of Rights*.

There have already been several judgements in South Africa that illustrate what these provisions mean: the Bhe and Shibi cases, which deal with succession and inheritance, the Gumede case which deals with marital property, and the Shilubana case which considers whether a woman can become chief. The IDRC-funded research was undertaken against the backdrop of this jurisprudence. It explored what was happening "on the ground" in areas where customary practices govern women's access to land. The South African survey found that the percentage of both never-married and widowed women, who were living on a residential plot that they themselves had acquired, was substantially higher for homesteads acquiring the land after 1994 (when South Africa's first post-apartheid election took place), than before 1994 at all three survey sites.

This finding seemed to contradict common assumptions about customary law — that it would deny "ownership" rights to women, especially single women. Given that the research was undertaken in ex-Bantustan areas, which are considered in legislation introduced by the post-1994 African National Congress government to be "traditional" communities, the finding might indeed seem to go against the Constitution's recognition of customary law.

However, South African Constitutional Court judgements have taken the view that customary law is "living law" rather than accepting the unchanged, codified version that was written down at some point in the past. The judgements referred to above accept that customary law can be flexible and that practices have changed over time. In the Bhe case, which overturned primogeniture (i.e., the exclusive right of inheritance of the firstborn son), the judgement asserted that "true customary law... recognises and acknowledges the changes which continually take place." In a judgement involving the mining company Alexkor, the court stated that "living" customary law is created when enough "people who live by its norms change their patterns of life." In the Shilubana case, which involved a daughter inheriting the chieftainship of her community after her father, the chief, died without a male heir, the court ruled in her favour, stating that "change is intrinsic to and can be invigorating of customary law."

The understanding that codified law misrepresents customary law and is, in fact, a colonial imposition was echoed by a member of parliament of Cameroon who attended the Nairobi symposium. The Hon. Joseph Mbah told the symposium,

> I'm a practising lawyer. I've hardly really been convinced of customary law as such. I prefer to talk of customs and usages because it's not easy to have a series of norms or rules that are applicable, positive rules. When you go into an African country, the first thing you face is the multiplicity of ethnic groups, with divergent niceties in the rules they apply, and proof of those rules is often an issue. [When you try to formalize law] you will realize that most of what we call customary laws are

On the web
THE RESEARCH

*actually interwoven with what the colonial masters brought in
at the time. So it's not easy to know what was custom and
what was instituted by the colonial masters.*

The Cameroon research report describes customary land tenure
as "characterized by its largely unwritten nature,... based on local
practices and norms, and... flexible, negotiable and location specific." The report notes further that customary practices differ
"slightly and sometimes significantly" among communities.
Similarly, the Mozambique research notes that customary law,
because it is not formalized, "may vary from one region to
another [and] from time to time."

Women's increasing ability to access land may not
represent a move toward gender equality, but instead
reflects the decreased importance attached to
agriculture as a form of livelihood.

One of the more controversial suggestions of the Cameroon
research report is that women's increasing ability to access land
may not represent a move toward gender equality, but instead
reflects the decreased importance attached to agriculture as a
form of livelihood. A similar argument can be made in South
Africa, where increased access to land by women actually represents increased access to what are generally small pieces of land
in the poverty-stricken former Bantustans where there is limited
economic potential.

The Cameroon report notes that, as increasing numbers of rural
men migrate to the cities or engage in non-farm income activities, women are likely, de facto, to be accorded greater control
and decision-making power over land and agricultural activities.
This trend makes it even more important to provide women
with the means — ranging from education to access to credit
and other economic resources — to perform these tasks, the
report adds.

Contesting "custom"

During the research on decentralization in Uganda, women participating in a focus group questioned whether the concept of "ownership" of land even exists in customary systems. They explained that their culture provides for trusteeship rather than ownership, i.e., land is held in trust for present and future generations (which is very different than thinking it can be bought and sold). According to focus group participants, men in Lira were "twisting the cultural meaning" by calling themselves "owners" of land. The land was communal, they said, for the use and benefit of both women and men, and men's rights relate only to trusteeship.

The women argued further that, while wives obtain land through their husband's kin groups, these groups have an obligation to protect the women's claims. They said that the abuse of women's land rights represents a failure of the male-led cultural institutions to carry out this duty. In both Lira and Mukono, women concurred that women have the right to land through a variety of social relationships. Women's claims to land are weak only in situations where male conspiracy is the order of the day, they said.

While not excusing the men involved, Dzodzi Tsikata, a research fellow at the Institute of Statistical, Social and Economic Research at the University of Ghana, observed that the reassertion of a women-unfriendly version of "traditional" land rights is understandable. It is, she believes, a reaction to policies and practices that have dispossessed many communities of their land to make way for national parks, conservation areas, plantations, mines, and other commercial developments.

Gaynor Paradza, who studied rural and urban planning at the University of Zimbabwe, suggests that a simple distinction

| Local gendered identities and citizenship
around land rights in Mukono and Lira, Uganda

The law sees men and women as equals, but the attitude is that land belongs to men:

Muwala – muvubuka – mukazi – mukyala; mulenzi – muvubuka – musajja – mutaka.
A woman's life cycle progresses from girl to adolescent, single woman, and "visitor" (married woman) whereas a man's life cycle progresses from boy to adolescent, man, and landlord. (In-depth key informant interview)

Mukyala means "visitor" (someone who came to visit. How can a visitor own land? (Focus group discussion, Area Land Committee)

Land belongs to men alone because women can move away anytime. (Focus group discussion, Area Land Committee)

Muttijjanabano. Abo bakyala, bajjakukyala (You fuss over women). Those women came to visit. This signifies women are accorded only access rights. (In-depth key informant interview)

Omukalasimutakansi; bijjabigereke. A woman is not a "landlord"; it is divinely ordained! (In-depth key informant interview)

I brought her alone (she came empty-handed without land); leave land alone. (Focus group discussion, Area Land Committee)

Under ancestral land tenure, land belongs to the clan and to the man. Land is passed on from generation to generation. (In-depth key informant interview)

The way the issue of co-ownership of family land has been perceived in Mukono is that in cases of divorce the woman takes half the land. Spousal co-ownership of land will increase instability in marriage as women will keep on marrying and divorcing up to five times to acquire land. If she marries and divorces five time she ends up owning more land than the men she has been married to. (In-depth key informant interview)

Source: Nakirunda (2011).

between customary (or what she terms "normative") and statutory laws is too simple (Paradza 2011a,b). Instead, there is a range of other arrangements that do not fall into either of these two categories, but are widely accepted as normal means of accessing land. These other arrangements "coexist with the state and traditional means, giving rise to a complex web of claims and opportunities and constraints to the stakeholders," she says. This observation raises the question of whether truly "customary" systems still exist in most African countries or whether, in turn, statutory systems can really be pure in form.

The prevalence of custom

The research projects offer strong evidence of the continuing relevance of custom. Such evidence is found in many forms, and the Malawi report (Banda et al. 2011) is one of the most explicit. The authors note that the *National Statistical Report* of 2004 indicates that 75% of the land in Malawi is "customary" land. As a result, most land transactions are guided by customary law.

The Cameroon report (Fonjong et al. 2009) contrasts the situation in urban and rural areas. Although land is traditionally inherited, owned, and managed by men, wealthy women in urban areas can and do purchase land freely. However, this is "unforeseeable" in rural areas because, in a family setting, men inherit the land and decide how it is to be used. This is despite the fact that the 1996 Constitution proclaims the right of ownership irrespective of gender.

In rural areas of Cameroon, a woman's access to land — let alone ownership — thus depends on a range of factors. These include age and marital status (including type and success of the marriage), whether the couple has children (and the number and sex of those children), and the woman's sexual conduct.

However, in many countries, there are opportunities within custom for women to access and control land. This possibility was the explicit focus of the research in South Africa (Budlender et al. 2011), but similar findings emerged in other countries, even where researchers started out with a negative view of the possibilities within custom.

THE RESEARCH
On the web

I liked the fact that there are some notions that I held that were put to test. One is the whole discussion about customary tenure and the fact that we always present it in a negative sense. But actually, when you see the way women seek to claim land rights, they are claiming inclusion rather than exclusionary control of land. And when you look at both registered land and customary land, customary land is more amenable to inclusionary land rights, whereas titled land is total exclusion. So as you move into individual registration and so on, you find that you are actually closing and enclosing more, and you are actually excluding more people, women inclusive.... So I started now interrogating my own assumptions. Josephine Ahikire, Centre for Basic Research, Uganda

The finding that there are opportunities and room to negotiate within customary law and practice is also supported by research among 22 single women in a communal area of Zimbabwe. According to Gaynor Paradza (2010, 2011a,b), changing customary tenure systems created opportunities for these women to negotiate access to land despite the common perception that single women are especially disadvantaged in relation to land rights. This finding mirrored that of the South African researchers, who found that single women — who constitute a growing proportion of the female population — were increasingly obtaining access to land in their own right.

Dzodzi Tsikata (2010) observes more generally that "contrary to the assumption that under customary law the individual's rights are clearly defined by their place and status within the kinship group, land relations are regularly renegotiated and contested, with outcomes reflecting the changing power relations within the landowning group."

In both Cameroon and South Africa, research provides evidence of how ways of acquiring land on some parts of the continent are changing and how customary and "modern" forms of land acquisition coexist even at the same site. In Cameroon, the principal land tenure system has shifted away from acquiring land through inheritance or traditional attribution to acquisition through purchase. Today almost 80% of land is purchased, and researchers suggest that this reflects a shift from customary to statutory practices in the regulation of land matters.

The research in South Africa allows for a comparison of modes (or routes) of acquiring homestead land before and after the first democratic elections of 1994. The mix of modes is perhaps even more complex in South Africa than elsewhere, given the multiple ways in which the colonial and subsequent apartheid systems attempted to restrict control of land by black people. According to the research, the percentage of residential land allocated by a chief or headman remained fairly constant before and after 1994: 42–45%. In contrast, acquisition through payment to a local leader almost tripled — from 9% to 26% — after 1994, while purchase increased from 2% to 6%. Payment to a local leader, the mode with the biggest percentage increase, represented what could be considered a hybrid mode, somewhere between custom and freehold purchase.

Coexistence of statutory and customary laws and practices

Given the coexistence of custom and statutory law in so many countries, the question arises as to how each of these systems might work to the advantage or disadvantage of particular groups of women.

The research in Uganda (Uganda Land Alliance and Uganda Media Women's Association 2010) built on the Uganda Land Alliance's previous inquiries into the practices of the administrator general's office with respect to inheritance rights. It had established that the central region of the country tended to have more cases of women inheriting land and matrimonial homes than other regions. This pattern was attributed to the fact that relatively few of the deceased from other regions had registered their land.

The new question addressed in the research was whether land reform had resulted in more ownership rights for women than traditional practices had accorded them. Follow-up interviews with female "clients" of the administrator general and interviews with subcounty chiefs, who play a key role in the land administration system, revealed that 45% of the women to whom the administrator general's office had granted letters of administration over inherited property still had the land. This was a higher percentage than that for men, as the latter were more likely to sell the land. Further, most of the women beneficiaries in the two targeted districts had decision-making power over the land.

Although these findings are positive in terms of women's rights, the research also revealed serious problems with the system that were unrelated to gender. For example, 4 of the 17 subcounty chiefs who were interviewed explained that provisions in the traditional and non-formal systems of inheritance, on one hand, and the conventional system, on the other, tended to contradict each other. They said that the contradictions caused confusion among beneficiaries and made resolution of cases difficult because different parties naturally wanted to apply the system that favoured their own interests.

Many women — both urban and rural — were unaware of the provisions of the statutory laws that give them rights over land. When women were asked why they had not applied for land registration, their answers suggested that customary practices still have a strong bearing on their perception of land ownership. More than a quarter of the women were unable to provide any valid reasons, while the remainder cited the cost of legal procedures and loyalty to customary practices. The researchers suggest that high rates of illiteracy among women (only 45% of women are literate as opposed to 67% of men) mean that they are less able to understand the importance of title deeds and engage in the land registration procedures.

The "loyalty" to customary practices found in Cameroon mirrors the comment of one of the Madagascar researchers concerning the influence of social and "emotional" aspects. Even when women have formal title to land, they might not claim the rights this affords them due to communal norms and power relations within the family.

> We thought that having a land certificate or land title would be enough to provide these women with secure access to the land. We didn't at all think about the social dimension and the issue of power relations within the household, within communities, that could substantially reduce women's security and their control on the land and its use. Mino Ramaroson, Harmonisation des Actions pour la Réalisation d'un Développement Intégré

Commonalities and differences among customary systems

Customary practices are not standard across African countries and communities. This book, and the IDRC-supported research more generally, emphasize the importance of exploring specific situations rather than perpetuating generalizations. Nevertheless, some commonalities merit attention both because of the strength of the "accepted wisdom" and because they often contain some element of truth.

For example, in many systems, women tend to move to their husband's area on marriage. Research in Malawi (Banda et al. 2011) comparing matrilineal (and matrilocal) and patrilineal systems shows that, although the practice is not universal, it is the most

On the web
THE RESEARCH

common. Further, the practice has implications in terms of women's control over land because communities are generally loath to give land to daughters on the grounds that they will marry and move away. Marriage, it is argued, means that the daughter's needs with respect to land will be looked after by the husband's family. Further, giving land to a daughter brings the risk that, on marriage, it would fall into the hands of another clan or grouping.

The Cameroon research report (Fonjong et al. 2009) quotes the paramount ruler of the Aghen people in Cameroon, who gave the following blunt explanation to researchers:

> *We have a reason why women cannot inherit land here, particularly because if the husband dies she can remarry, and by remarrying she can do anything with the land which perhaps was a family property. Our native law forbids a woman from inheriting land. We cannot allow her because she will normally remarry. In so doing, family land will get to that other man and the man now can do anything with the land.*

Similarly, a summary of the research conducted by the Makerere Institute of Social Research (2010) in Uganda, Rwanda, and Kenya notes that, although the legal frameworks in all three countries recognize and provide for equal inheritance by male and female children, "in practice, females are sidelined with the excuse that they have left (or will leave) the natal family to start another."

The reasons for preventing women from acquiring control over land could be argued to be weaker with respect to widows. Indeed, Kenya's *Law of Succession Act* (Kenya 1981) provides that a woman can inherit land and other property from her husband's estate. However, research suggests that inheritance is often contested, especially in the case of younger women widowed as a result of AIDS. In these cases, the argument is offered again that the woman might well remarry a man from another clan or grouping, in which case the land would fall under the control of an outsider.

> To what extent, then, are widows "choosing" not to pursue their rights in the face of social pressure rather than being forcibly dispossessed of land?

In land disputes involving widows in Kenya (Young Widows Advancement Program 2011), 84% of the women said that their in-laws were the other parties in the conflict. Even disregarding the increase in numbers of younger widows, this suggests that reluctance to grant widows control over land is not restricted to cases where they might remarry. It would be wrong, however, to leap to the conclusion that the restrictions on female inheritance are the main constraint to women's control over land. In-laws are not the only opponents to women's claims to land.

In Rwanda (Rwanda Women's Network 2011), "other parties" to 40 disputes in which women were involved included 15 neighbours, 10 spouses, and 9 siblings. In only six cases were in-laws named as the contesting parties. Although the number of cases involving in-laws is small, the Rwandan researchers argue that the fact that most disputants were connected to the woman complainant is an indication of the continuation of customary practices and perceptions regarding women's land rights. The researchers also suggest that cases where their own children are named as disputants imply greater vulnerability of aging women.

On the web
THE RESEARCH

Force of law or social pressure?

The reluctance of women in Cameroon to press their land claims suggests that not only formal laws but also social pressures are a factor. To what extent, then, are widows "choosing" not to pursue their rights in the face of social pressure rather than being forcibly dispossessed of land?

In Kenya, participants in the research conducted by the Young Widows Advancement Program (2011) provide at least a partial answer. Some reported that in-laws "gang up together against you and push you to the wall." In this situation, many women might "choose" to leave. One widow told researchers: "I had to leave so that I could get peace of mind. I just want to look after my children."

The South African questionnaire (Budlender et al. 2011) included questions about eviction framed in a way that aimed to capture both the forced and "chosen" evictions. Much thought was given to this issue in the design of the questionnaire after a local organization at one site pointed out that the wording of this question would affect the results.

Thus, the survey began by asking whether the woman had ever personally lost access to, or had to leave, any of a range of types of land such as the residential plot, garden plot, and fields. Women who answered yes were then asked for the main reason why this had happened. The response options were: "I felt forced to move because of bad relationships," "I chose to move to a better alternative but was not forced to move," "I was threatened with eviction," and "I was evicted." She was also asked to name who was mainly responsible for her having to leave or being threatened.

Of the full sample of 3,000, just 115 women (3.8%) reported that they had lost access to, or had to leave, a residential plot. Of these, 31 said that they were evicted, with a further 7 reporting that they were threatened with eviction. A further 32 felt forced to move because of bad relationships, while a similar number had voluntarily moved to a better alternative

Matrilineal and patrilineal systems in Malawi

Although there are some similarities among customary systems in much of Africa, there are also variations. Malawi presents an interesting case in that it includes both patrilineal systems and the more unusual matrilineal system. The sites for the IDRC-funded research (Banda et al. 2011) were chosen to allow for comparison between the two.

The researchers found, as expected, that women's control over land was restricted in a patrilineal system. In general, women had control only over small "kitchen gardens," whereas larger pieces of land, on which cash crops were grown, were controlled by their husbands.

A woman's supposed tenured security in matrilineal
societies is less secure than might be expected.

Women in the matrilineal system asserted that they had greater control. However, after probing further, the researchers found that the women were obliged to consult their maternal uncle or husband regarding some of the more important decisions. For example, women were not free to sell or lease out their land without such consultation. Married women in a matrilineal system were also said to allow men to decide what crops to grow. The reason offered for this practice, despite the woman being the "owner," was that the man had the "economic means."

According to the research, a woman's supposed tenured security in matrilineal societies is less secure than might be expected. With increasing pressure on land due to commercialization, "the same uncles that are supposed to protect women are now the ones that are actually abusers." Cases were reported of uncles taking land away from women to sell it to investors or use it for other purposes. However, in comparison with the patrilineal system, matrilineal societies include some positive customs, which if followed could foster greater opportunities for women. For example, individual women can be considered owners of land whether or not they are married.

Challenging regressive practices in court

For the most part, the IDRC-funded research was done by, or in collaboration with, organizations that are working with or supporting women in rural areas. Many of them have come up with innovative ways to challenge the discrimination and other obstacles facing women in relation to land. Some of these initiatives assist individual women, for example, by providing legal advice. Others attempt to tackle the problems more systemically, for example, by instituting legal court challenges. These two approaches can often complement each other.

One of the primary reasons for embarking on the South African research was to obtain solid evidence that could be used in court challenges of discriminatory practices. As discussed above, several constitutional court cases have incorporated progressive and rights-based understanding of customary law, arguing that the progressive interpretation reflects changes that have occurred in "living" law. In community consultation meetings around proposed legislation, many women and men spoke about how women are increasingly gaining access to land in many parts of the country. However, when those opposing the new legislation attempted to use these stories as evidence in a court challenge, the evidence was rejected on the basis that it was anecdotal. The researchers hoped that a large-scale survey would provide evidence that was more difficult to reject.

South Africa is not the only African country in which court challenges have been used to promote gender equality. The Cameroon report (Fonjong et al. 2009) cites the Supreme Court case of *Zamcho Florence Lum v. Chibikom Peter Fru & others*, and the High Court Meme Case of *David Tchakokam v. Koeu Magdalene*.

So the judges have been making these progressive, radical decisions in courts in favour of women and land. I think it is through these progressive judges that we're going to continue recruiting, to help us see how to weaken customary law. In Tanzania, there is a procedure for changing customary law, but who knows about it? It is only the lawyers, and male lawyers at that. So if female lawyers can lead everybody else to interact with customary law because the law says, if you want to change customary law, you need 100 signatures and say what is wrong with an aspect of customary law. Once you get 100 signatures, then a lawyer can bring this to question, and a discussion begins in that community. Magdalene Ngaiza, University of Dar es Salaam

Interplay of marital and land laws

Marital status is important in determining access to and control over land. This is an area in which customary, civil, and religious laws and customs interact in different ways across countries. Often particular marital regimes and forms confer superior rights compared with other laws, including land laws.

Rwanda has attempted to address the problem of unequal rights by recognizing only monogamous civil marriage. Within this form of marriage, the law explicitly provides for equal rights and duties of husband and wife during marriage and divorce. The objectives of this law are to prevent multiple relationships, to streamline property rights in marriage, and to protect children.

The Rwanda research report notes that while the new laws have enhanced property rights for women in monogamous civil marriages, a large number of women still cohabit or are in a polygamous marriage. Among the 50 women involved in land disputes who were followed in the research, almost half were in traditional marriages or were widows of traditional marriages. As the researchers note, the fact that many women entered into marital unions before the legal reforms were introduced implies that simply enacting laws cannot bring about an immediate change from customary to statutory practices.

On the web
THE RESEARCH

> The Rwanda research report notes that while new laws
> have enhanced property rights for women in monog-
> amous civil marriages, a large number of women still
> cohabit or are in a polygamous marriage.

The effect of decentralization

Comparative research in Uganda, Tanzania, and Kenya focused
on three issues: decentralization of land administration systems
and how they shape women's entitlements; the emerging cultural
and political trends vis-à-vis women's land claims; and women's
organization and capacity to engage with institutions of power at
local levels.

In Uganda, researchers from the Centre for Basic Research (CBR)
found that, although women have a presence in local administration, their roles and visibility are limited (Ahikire 2011). In very
few cases have they been able to play a critical role in decision-
making at the district level. At the same time, little use has been
made of the *Land Act* "consent clause" (Uganda 1998). This
offers legal recognition of women's rights, but there is no clarity
on what mechanisms are needed for its enforcement, and few
citizens have any knowledge of it.

Decentralization of land administration and management in
Uganda has been accompanied by localization of mechanisms to
resolve land disputes. However, the CBR's research indicates that
several land dispute resolution institutions coexist without clear
coordination mechanisms. Parties to land disputes often engage
in "forum shopping" — choosing the channels they deem more
favourable to their cause at a particular point. These include: the
Chief Magistrate's Local Council II and III Courts, family and
clans, resident district commissioners, and district land boards.

Disputes over land can have many causes. They range from the commonplace, such as boundary disputes, trespassing, and multiple sales of the same land, to the unforeseen, such as a case where an owner lent land to a friend and both subsequently died, leaving their children to fight over the land. However, decentralized land systems have provided some benefits to women. For example, local council courts are said to have created an opening for increased engagement with women and to be more "humane" and less formal than the magistrate's court.

The CBR's research notes that culture is often twisted "in the name of protection." In Uganda, for example, there is general consensus in Lira and Mukono that women get land through social relations; therefore, women's claims on land are weak only where there is a male conspiracy to keep them that way. Decentralization offers opportunities for women to serve on land administration bodies, providing a deterrent to abuse and denial of land rights. However, apart from isolated cases of women in politics being supportive, decentralization has not led to significant gains for women.

Tanzania operates under a dual system centralized at the Ministry of Lands, Housing and Human Settlement Development and in district land offices that are under the Prime Minister's Office — Regional Administration and Local Government. At the local level, village councils are responsible for managing village land and other property on behalf of beneficiaries. The councils also act as dispute resolution bodies, while village adjudication committees determine boundaries. The *Village Land Act, 1999* provides for affirmative action for women in that it reserves 25% of the seats on all local structures for women (Tanzania 1999). However, participation by women has not yet affected women's land rights in a positive way.

On the web

THE RESEARCH

The Tanzanian research concludes that, although the legal framework provides for equality of access and ownership of land, the mechanisms and practice still sustain male dominance in land administration. As in Uganda, conflict resolution mechanisms for land are cumbersome and unclear, and there is little knowledge of what the laws entail in terms of land administration.

Research undertaken by the University of Nairobi in collaboration with the CBR takes into account the new Kenyan Constitution, which was approved by referendum in 2010 and provides a model of decentralized land administration that differs from concepts that were on the table in earlier referendum discussions. For example, in previous draft constitutions, districts were the main unit of devolution within five tiers of government. The new Constitution provides for a two-tier system of national and county governments.

A key goal for the 47 county governments is to give the people power for self-governance and enhance their participation in their development process. Further, the county governments are meant to facilitate the decentralization of state organs, functions, and services to the local level. Each county will be headed by a governor, and Article 175(c) of the Constitution provides that "no more than two-thirds of the members of representative bodies in each county government shall be of the same gender."

> Female membership on land control boards has led to a change in the public perception that land matters are exclusively a male domain.

Even before adoption of the new Kenyan Constitution, land control boards were established to regulate transactions involving agricultural land. Located in each administrative district or division, these boards are potentially important in helping women assert their land rights, but few members of the public are even aware of their existence. Only 54 of 160 respondents surveyed had ever heard of the land control board. Awareness varied among the districts studied: in Nyeri, 60% of those sampled were aware of the boards, but only 20% in Kitui and Kwale. When asked about the functions of the land control board, respondents revealed very little knowledge of their role. Only 20% had ever sought the board's services.

Except for ministry appointees, recruitment for membership on the land control boards has involved an advertisement in the district, divisional, and local offices calling for interested candidates, with women being encouraged to participate. Women applicants in Nyeri are almost on par with men in terms of education and experience, and female membership on land control boards has led to a change in the public perception that land matters are exclusively a male domain.

Women board members have begun to examine critically the cases of men who come to the boards seeking consent to sell part of the family land. Boards in the three districts have now made it a rule that anybody seeking to dispose of family land must demonstrate spousal approval, as well as that of children. The board uses a variety of techniques to ascertain the authenticity of the spouses. In Nyeri, it was reported, one man had tried to cheat the land control board by bringing a call girl to give consent to sell family land. However, with the help of local people, the board was able to establish that the man wanted to sell part of the family land without involving his wife. Ten years ago, he would have been able to do this, but no longer.

National land policies and reforms

Dzodzi Tsikata (2010) notes that there are several common ways in which legislation has attempted to prevent a disadvantage to women in terms of ownership of, and control over, land. These include joint registration of land by spouses, requiring spousal consent for land sales, and providing for representation of women in local land administration institutions, possibly through quotas. She also notes that, although these interventions are important, they would not result in fundamental change in land tenure systems, given the increasing hunger for land and loss of tenure security. This is because these interventions with respect to gender equality are embedded in broader market liberalization reforms related to land administration institutions, land legislation, adjudication, titling, and registration of land rights. The aim of all those reforms is to "strengthen land markets and make them more efficient and convenient for foreign investors with trickle-down benefits for locals."

Although Tsikata's warning is pertinent, it can be argued that these interventions could play a part in ensuring that women benefit equitably to the extent land is available. Thus, it is important to investigate to what extent the common interventions actually make a difference on the ground.

Spousal consent

Uganda's *Land (Amendment) Act* (Uganda 2004) specifies that a married man (or, less often, woman) must obtain the consent of the spouse before engaging in any transactions involving the family land. It adds that any transaction executed in breach of this clause is null and void. Research conducted by the Foundation for Human Rights Initiative in Uganda investigated the extent to which this spousal consent clause is being observed (Kabugo et al. 2011). In the two subcounties where research was conducted, a local human rights organization had received reports from 129 women who were either evicted by buyers of family land sold by their husbands without the wives' consent or were living in fear of being evicted in this way. The foundation's own records suggested that, in 2007, about half of reported land cases related to violation of the spousal consent clause.

The researchers found that 37 of the 40 respondents who answered the question knew that husbands must obtain their wife's consent before selling family land. This might be an over-estimate of knowledge among the general population, however, given the method used to select respondents. In focus group discussions, no participants other than government officials named the spousal consent clause.

Participants in the focus groups also had a different understanding of the term "spouse" than that enshrined in law. Most considered that a man and woman who live together and have children are spouses. Yet in Ugandan law the term "spouse" refers only to those who are legally married. This is a problem in that the researchers claim that most of the couples in the two subcounties where the research was conducted, as in other rural areas, are not legally married. A high incidence of cohabitation was reported by the Uganda Rural Development and Training Programme (2011), which notes that "quasi-polygamy" is the most prevalent form of marriage, where a man marries one woman customarily, but continues to cohabit with one or more other women.

Kabugo et al. (2011) note that when the legal meaning of "spouse" was pointed out to participants in the focus groups, the participants "were left wondering if the law is actually addressing the issue of women's access and control over land." However, although this comment suggests that participants supported what the law was trying to achieve, the research also quotes a 20-year-old man who was not in favour. He commented, "When I wed my wife she also becomes part of my property and, therefore, I can deal with my property the way I want to, including the family land."

Further, most participants felt that even lawfully married women should not be entitled if they had not borne children, as children were a necessary component of the institution of marriage.

Because the land laws have been passed a decade ago, we were surprised when we interviewed women in the rural area, in the village, for a woman to stand up and say that, "For me to go and register my own name in the process of land allocation, that will be disrespectful. I have to register my husband's name because the land will be for my sons".... And then another respondent, a male, said categorically that, "Customary land, I am the one who inherited. My sisters can use the land but they cannot inherit. I'm like a king." Josephine Ahikire, Centre for Basic Research, Uganda

Promotion and protection of inheritance and succession rights

Since 1999, Rwanda has had a progressive statutory regime that recognizes and protects women's right to own and inherit land. This regime includes the 1999 inheritance and succession law (Rwanda 1999), which complements the institutionalization of various matrimonial regimes under the 1960 *Civil Code*. The inheritance and succession law explicitly grants equal inheritance rights to male and female children and allows a wife to inherit her deceased husband's property.

These laws operate in tandem with the National Land Policy (Rwanda 2004) and the Organic Land Law (Rwanda 2005). The policy and law are intended to enhance the tenure security of ordinary Rwandans by giving them rights to long-term lease (99 years, renewable) of their land and stipulating that all land in Rwanda must be formally registered. Further, the law stipulates that land rights cannot be transferred without the consent of all family members, including legally married spouses and adult children. (Rwanda's law also currently recognizes only monogamous civil marriages.) Consent is provided by submitting a document signed by the family members to a registrar of civil status or the land registrar.

Research by the Rwanda Women's Network (2011) was designed to investigate to what extent these legal reforms had influenced practices on the ground. The researchers traced 50 women out of a total of 147 who were recorded as having reported cases to the court and the *Abunzi* (a long-standing system of community volunteers who assist in resolving disputes). Information obtained from interviews with the 50 women and with land administrators revealed that customary inheritance practices were still widespread alongside the new legislation. Furthermore, most disputes involving women were resolved by the *Abunzi*, who operate outside the traditional councils.

We've got what we call mediators – they're called Abunzi in Kinyarwanda – because we already had these people, this group of people in our culture whereby... this group was composed of old people who could sit down and get what is taking place in the community.... So this is the system we had to bring back. But these people, they are not even paid, they do this voluntarily. And... which is more complicated is that they don't have materials, I mean, the copies of the different laws because they do face different cases. You could find that they don't have land law, they don't have succession law, they don't have inheritance law, they don't have registration law. So it's just how they are trying to address these disputes without having that. So the findings did reveal that there is a lack of all this material that they need just to help them address. And what we found out was, it's as if [the women] are thinking that having access to land is a favour, it's not a right for them. Odeth Kantengwa, Rwanda Women's Network

Women chose the *Abunzi* as they felt that the alternative systems provided for in the laws of the family council and the *umudugudu* (village) were biased and susceptible to corruption. They felt that the *Abunzi* tended to follow the law, while this was not the case with the other institutions. Although women were increasingly aware of their land rights, they faced a number of challenges and lacked assistance in asserting and pursuing those rights.

Informal non-legal approaches

The GROOTS initiative in Kenya represents another non-traditional innovation introduced by a civil society organization to address the problems faced by AIDS widows and orphans in relation to land and other rights. GROOTS Kenya initiated its approach after observing that many HIV-positive widows were thrown out of their matrimonial homes and their land was confiscated as they were blamed for the death of their husbands. In Gatundu, where the IDRC-funded research was conducted, many of these cases were encountered by volunteer home-based caregivers who were members of GROOTS.

In response, GROOTS began assisting communities to establish community land and property watch dog groups (WDGs), which brought together home-based caregivers, paralegals, and elders, as well as religious and local government leaders to safeguard women's land rights. The WDGs use a range of strategies, including reporting cases of dispossession of property to local traditional leaders, informing women of their legal rights, and mediating and assisting them to enforce land claims. They also lobby land administrators to demand letters showing spousal consent for land transactions.

The groups have been accepted by the authorities to the extent that they are represented on formal decision-making fora that adjudicate land disputes and transactions. Most of the cases reviewed in the GROOTS (2011) research project were reported by women (58.8%) rather than men (37.6%), possibly because most of the victims were women or children (3.6% of the cases reported were unclear). Figure 1 shows the demographics of property victims in Gatundu District.

The WDG initiative has achieved gains for individual women, as well as at the broader community level. There are also cases where the intervention of a WDG has led to the dismissal of corrupt local government officials who were taking advantage of women. However, although these achievements are impressive, there are limitations to the initiative. Sometimes the WDG members themselves lack the necessary knowledge and skills to carry out the wide range of tasks envisaged for the groups. Further, the fact that the system relies on volunteers raises questions about both sustainability and fairness, given that incumbents of other institutions dealing with these issues are paid professionals.

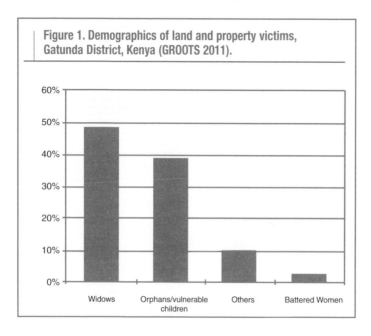

Figure 1. Demographics of land and property victims, Gatunda District, Kenya (GROOTS 2011).

Comparing the impact of customary and statutory processes

In Madagascar, researchers attempted to compare women's access to land under customary and reformed statutory processes. Land in Madagascar is subject to a range of tenure systems. Only about 10% is registered and privately owned based on French property law. Most of the remainder, although presumed in law to be owned by the state, is in fact occupied by those on whom ownership has been conferred through locally legitimated processes derived from custom.

Until recently, few Madagascar citizens resorted to registration as they felt secure in their customary rights. However, in 2005, the government declared a land tenure crisis, which was said to be having serious economic and social consequences. In particular, it had supposedly led to reluctance of the private sector and farmers to invest in their land.

A new land policy was announced aimed at promoting secure access to land by creating a more efficient, decentralized land management system. The new policy afforded legal recognition to ownership derived from occupation and use. It integrated local, traditional structures (the village elders) and decentralized municipal structures into the process of recognition. Local land offices were established and given responsibility for registering non-titled private property and issuing land certificates.

This was the background for an IDRC-supported research project (Ramaroson et al. 2011) that aimed to understand what factors affected women's access to land certificates. The need for this research was heightened by a political crisis in late 2008 sparked by an increase in land sales, including the sale of large areas of occupied state-owned land to external investors.

The research was conducted at two sites, Miadanandriana and Sahambavy. In Miadanandriana, the researchers found that inheritance practices had changed. Interviews and focus group discussions revealed that, in this area, most women and men inherited from their parents. Men and women had the same rights and, therefore, received the same amount and types of land. The researchers noted that, although the site is rural, it is located near the capital where there is easy access to social services such as education and information. The population in this region, therefore, had better knowledge of the laws than elsewhere, and this might have contributed to what the researchers termed "loss of cultural identity."

In Sahambavy, inheritance was shaped primarily by customary practices. Women could inherit, but the size and type of land they acquired would not be the same as that of men. Women would receive a small, symbolic portion of the inherited land, termed *sotroihinanana* (literally — small spoon for eating). The rest of the land they inherited would be given to their brothers, who would be responsible for all social obligations in the village. However, if the woman returned to the family village after being widowed or divorced, she would be able to claim access to this land. A legally married woman who purchased land with her husband would get half if they divorced or she was widowed. A woman who married through customary practices would receive only a third of such land.

The research revealed that only 8 of the 59 land certificates issued by the local land office were in the name of a women. Women reported that the procedure for obtaining land certificates was long and expensive and they did not have the time or money to undertake such applications. However, the researchers did not find any correlation between wealth and ownership of a land certificate. Many women stated that land issues, such as titles and registration, are men's concerns.

On the web

THE RESEARCH

Ignorance of the law

The Madagascar researchers, like those in several other countries, remark on the high levels of ignorance of the statutory laws and reforms. Several of the research initiatives found that ignorance was not confined to women who were potential beneficiaries. The Rwanda research highlights similar lack of knowledge, as well as lack of access to the necessary documents, on the part of the *Abunzi*, who still mediate many land disputes. In Malawi, a roundtable discussion with chiefs revealed that most of them lacked sufficient knowledge of statutory laws relating to land.

This led to their reliance on customary laws which had been in effect "since time immemorial." In Uganda, the research on decentralization revealed that even district officials did not have comprehensive knowledge of land legislation.

These findings might seem to support the policy proposals and recommendations to "educate" women and other actors that some of the research reports contain. However, there is evidence that general education is unlikely to have a major impact. For example, in Madagascar, the level of women's education did not appear to influence whether they had visited the local land office in Miadanandriana. In Rwanda, 20 of the 50 women interviewed were unable to read in either official languages (French or Kinyarwanda); yet these women had pursued their land rights in formal institutions.

Tsikata (2010) questions how much even targeted legal education and paralegal training can achieve, noting the amount of time and resources that have been invested in these activities over recent years: "No doubt some women have been empowered to struggle for their rights because of a growing awareness of what laws have been passed. However, the stress on legal education displaces the power issues which are central in the inequalities."

The cost of accessing formal legal processes

Even where women are aware of progressive laws, the cost (in both money and time) of taking advantage of these laws is often prohibitive. In Kenya, where all land is meant to be registered, many widows struggle to find the money necessary to search for their property documents at the deeds registry (GROOTS 2011). Women were also required to pay court filing and disbursement fees.

The initial process of freezing any land transaction also required paying a fee to lodge a "caution of restriction." Further, although the rules provide for waiving of court fees for low-income applicants, the application for such a waiver also requires a fee! In terms of time, one of the women leaders reported walking three hours to the local court, sometimes only to find that the matter did not proceed.

In Uganda, members of Local Council 2 are not remunerated. As a result, these councils, which constitute the first port of call in relation to land disputes, tend to see court fees as a way of raising revenue.

In Rwanda, women also face a cumbersome process in meeting all the legal requirements, and 21 of the women surveyed said that they had limited knowledge of the laws. The amount of time required to pursue legal processes was particularly challenging given the many responsibilities of women in the household. These challenges are compounded by fear of physical violence by family members reported by 25 of the 50 women.

Women's claims in a context of "economic development"

For the most part, the IDRC-funded research focused on access to and ownership of land; several other important research questions were not dealt with in-depth and could be fertile topics for future inquiry. For example, in what specific ways was land used, and how did that contribute to economic development and how have broader macroeconomic and related developments contributed to the creation of the current social contexts for women's struggles to gain access to land?

These types of concerns, revolving around the broader economic and political circumstances that frame discussions of women and land, were touched on by a few of the projects. In Cameroon, for example, the researchers made some enlightening comparisons between the country's current economic conditions and those that existed historically. They note that today's intense competition for land has complicated the prospects of women attempting to access that land. Current-day free market land policies, combined with a patriarchal system that does not recognize women's roles as farmers or landowners, have put women in a more difficult position than they occupied in pre-colonial Cameroon. Although the pre-colonial communal land system ensured that women, as a more integral part of the community, were provided for and provided with meaningful roles, today they are more likely to be dispossessed from land.

Furthermore, the rise of coffee as a cash crop and the shift away from subsistence farming to cash cropping promoted by the Operation Green Revolution strategy of the 1970s have also worked against women. Both these trends have increased the monetary value of land, resulting in men sometimes "confiscating" fertile lands that had been controlled by wives or sisters.

The Mozambican researchers also took a "big picture" approach, investigating the conflict between commercial agriculture and small-scale subsistence farming (Andrade et al. 2009). In the community of Maragra near Manhiça village, they focused on approximately 50 women, most of whom were employed through seasonal contracts in the cane plantations of the powerful Maragra sugar company. Most of the women were originally immigrants from Cabo-Delgado province and, as a result, they have to rent land from local people to cultivate for themselves.

These women, who face disadvantages stemming from their gender, class, and place of origin, have worked to change their circumstances by creating a cooperative that includes both individual farms and a collective farm. With this as their base, they are attempting to claim rights, as well as access to tractors and other inputs needed for their subsistence agriculture enterprise.

Table 2. Comparison of women's access to and use of land in poor and wealthy households.

	Crop					
	Eucalyptus (forest)	Sweet potatoes (farmyard garden)	Cassava (upland crop)	Legumes (baiboho)	Rice (lowland crop)	Potatoes, beans (lowland, off-season crops)
Poor households						
Activities	Collect firewood	Plant, weed, harvest	Plant, weed	Weed, harvest	Weed, storage	All except land preparation
Procedure used to access land	Accepted by the community	Inherited by husband	Inherited by husband	Inherited by husband	Inherited by husband	Inherited by husband
Control over produce	+++ (household use)	++	Household consumption	+	Men sell Women use for household consumption	+
Wealthy households						
Activities	Non-applicable; charcoal or firewood is purchased	Harvest		Weed, harvest	Use external labour and mutual aid	Use external labour and mutual aid
Procedure used to access land	Purchased	Inherited by husband		Inherited by husband	Inherited by husband and acquired by the couple	Inherited by husband and acquired by the couple
Control over produce		+++	++	+++	++ (couple)	++ (couple)

Note: +, low level of control; ++, medium level of control +++, high level of control.

How land is used: the micro picture

In Madagascar, the researchers used a range of methods, including participatory rural appraisal, to explore the roles played by women and men in agriculture (Ramaroson et al. 2011). The team carefully distinguished among activities reported for poor, medium-income, and wealthy households, highlighting not only differences in tasks, but also differences in the relative power of women and men in these three groups.

Table 2 highlights some of the distinctions in terms of women's access to and use of land by class. Women in poor households have access to land, but very limited control over it. Men decide which crops to grow, even though women do the hard work. Women can decide on the use of produce from the farmyard garden, *baiboho*, and lowlands (but for off-season cropping) — to sell or use it for household consumption. However, the men decide how to use the money obtained from crop sales. Poor women also work as labourers on other people's plots to generate income.

In contrast, wealthy women have more control over the land they use. They work less than other classes of women and have more say in decision-making. In fact, their husbands often consult them about what to do with the crops. These families have enough produce to sell, in addition to what they need for household consumption. They can also often afford to buy rice fields or other types of land. In these cases, women have more rights to land, as much of it has not been inherited from the husband's family.

The researchers noted that the rights of both poor and medium-income women to collect firewood from forest areas is recognized, even though the land is not owned by the women or, indeed, by their families.

In Zimbabwe, the researchers aimed to go beyond the issue of access to land to investigate whether and how women, who accessed land through the Fast Track Land Reform Programme introduced in 2000, were able to report successful production eight years later (Mazhawidza and Manjenwa 2011). During one of the planning meetings, the team leader explained that this focus was necessary because women face challenges in obtaining farming equipment and other inputs necessary to use the land.

The research confirmed earlier reports that found that many women who took part in the *jambanja* land invasions of 1999–2000 did not gain access to land. (*Jambanja* is a Zimbabwean term describing the disorder or chaos of the time.) Furthermore, many women were among those who lost jobs (and sometimes homes) as permanent or casual workers on commercial farms. The researchers also noted that the Fast Track Land Reform Programme led to decreased availability of firewood, forcing women to travel further and spend longer hours collecting fuel.

> "At least now I have somewhere to be buried. If you are looking for me, you know where to find me."

The team leader argued that it was of little use to question the policy eight years after the fact, as the allocations were a "done deal." Also, given that land ownership is one of the most highly politicized issues in the country, questioning the allocation might not be wise. Instead, the research focused on cases of women who had been successful in securing resettlement land through allocation of plots by the district administrator of the Ministry of Lands.

The report notes that when land was being redistributed, the national women's network asked that 20% of the land be allocated to women. The Presidential Land Review Committee of 2003 found that 18% of A1 (village-owned and operated, rather than commercial) land was allocated to women in their own right. The researchers contrast this with the fact that women account for about 65% of the rural population, but acknowledge

On the web
THE RESEARCH

that many of these women obtained land through marriage. The follow-up IDRC-funded research aimed to investigate the social, economic, and political issues for women who obtained land in their own right.

Although the sample was far too small to provide nationally representative findings, the responses of several women illustrate how the importance of land extends beyond the economic. One noted, "Land is food, land is dignity, and land is economic empowerment." Another spoke about dignity, saying, "At least now I have somewhere to be buried. If you are looking for me, you know where to find me."

Part 4

Lessons learned

Lessons about research

A wide range of research methods was used across the various country studies. The South African research involved a standard-ized survey administered to 3,000 randomly selected adult women at three sites. This was complemented by focus group discussions at each site, before and after the survey. Similarly, the Cameroon research included a large-scale survey of women and men, as well as interviews and discussion groups. The interviewees encompassed individuals from all socioeconomic, political, demographic, and ethnic groups within the study area.

Many of the other research projects relied heavily on qualitative methods, such as focus groups and in-depth interviews, especially those funded through small grants. Some also included surveys, but these were generally small-scale in terms of sample size.

Several projects employed non-traditional research approaches. For example, the Madagascar team used participatory rural appraisal techniques. Even more unusual, "appreciative enquiry" was used in the Uganda Rural Development and Training Program's research, in line with the researchers' "visionary approach" to rural development, which attempts to enable

On the web **THE LESSONS**

women to view critically and evolve their own individual and community aspirations regarding land.

Those with a narrow conception of what constitutes "proper" research might be concerned about how these non-traditional approaches could skew findings. The clear advantage of these participation-oriented research methods is their potential to bring about more immediate benefits than other methods might yield. For example, in the Uganda case, the women involved in the visioning workshops subsequently established a savings group and other collective initiatives to address the problems they had discussed. Similarly, in Mozambique the research contributed to the establishment of a legal assistance program in which a community-based organization provides legal assistance to women whose rights have been violated in areas that include family law, land law, and domestic violence. Women also established a cooperative to assist in protecting their collective and individual land from being used for cane production.

In Malawi, the research report includes the following among the "key innovative practices" used in or subsequent to the research:

➤ Working with customary leaders in the patrilineal society of Mzimba, resulting in chiefs speaking out against land dispossession which widows experience.

➤ Creation of women's advocacy groups, which support women's agency. In Mzimba, the women's groups that were established have been networking with the Coalition of Women Farmers. With organizational help from the NGO Action Aid, these women's organizations together have been engaging with customary leaders, in an effort to claim their land rights.

One of the challenges of involving activist organizations in the research is striking an appropriate balance among documentation, advocacy, and research. Participatory researchers may sometimes appear more concerned with achieving practical advances than with generating new knowledge. However, as Sabine Pallas of the ILC notes, the success and continuation of research that involves disadvantaged people depend on their realization of some tangible gains:

> *It's really a very challenging task to link the people who are doing the research and the people who are living this type of situation in their daily life, because they speak different languages, different registers of language, and sometimes it's not so easy to make the connection between the two.... We've started doing that through this project and we've built a lot of relationships... otherwise you run the risk that the research is very rigorous and of great academic quality and you can publish it in a journal — but will it actually be useful for the people?*

Policy conclusions

Virtually all the IDRC-funded studies focused on particular areas of a particular country. Therefore, we should be cautious about extracting general lessons — given the variations in local circumstances. However, one clear commonality is that greater numbers of women appear to be gaining access to land than in the past. This provokes the subsequent question, however, of whether this is an entirely positive development or whether at least some of the gains might reflect the fact that more men have left for "greener pastures" in the cities, leaving women with access to a less-useful resource. The studies from Cameroon and South Africa might support the latter suggestion.

The research provided evidence of a range of legal and other reforms that aim to promote gender equality, often alongside other objectives. However, in most cases, these were patchily implemented or had limited effects. Merely passing legislation is of little use if the necessary resources for implementation are not

On the web

THE LESSONS

provided, if all relevant actors are not informed and educated on the provisions, if the reforms are not monitored, and if there are no effective sanctions for failure to implement. Further, more careful thought is needed during the design of reforms and regarding monitoring of their implementation. As Tsikata (2010) warns, the sometimes simplistic "solutions" legislated to date — such as joint titling or representation of women on land administration bodies — are of limited effectiveness.

The IDRC-funded research, with its emphasis on hearing the voices of women on the ground, highlights the importance of consulting and involving women when designing reforms and monitoring implementation. Monitoring will provide a more accurate picture if it involves learning about women's actual experiences, rather than simply consulting administrative records or conducting interviews with officials.

> *Just being with the communities refreshes my ideas on law because it's so easy, as a lawyer, to just talk about what entitlements are. But many times when you do this kind of research, you come back and you say: "But hang on, when you look at these women, for them it's not about the right provided for in the law; it is about whether there's food on the table." So you have to link whatever policy and legal issues there are to very practical things on a day-to-day basis.* Patricia Kameri-Mbote, University of Nairobi

Across all countries, the research confirms that women's access to land does not simply hinge on a choice between customary and statutory systems. Rather, we are faced with a more complex question of how the two systems interact and are used by different groups of women and men. The research highlights the "flexibility" of customary law and practices.

There are both negatives and positives to be found in these research reports. On the negative side, the research shows how custom can be used to subvert well-intentioned statutory provisions and the persistent challenge to enforce laws. On the more positive side, it is clear that, in some countries, customs have been successfully adapted to fit changing situations. The research thus emphasizes the need to start thinking about customary law as living and evolving, rather than something that will forever retain the form that was written down or formalized by past colonial administrators and anthropologists.

The politicized nature of land

Finally, it is important to recognize the highly politicized nature of land questions in many parts of Africa. This point was highlighted by researchers at one organization, who warned that if the research findings were used to discredit the government in the eyes of international donors, it could undermine the work done by their organization — or threaten its very existence.

Two of the Uganda research teams reported more local-level challenges to the research resulting from sensitivity around land issues. The Uganda Rural Development and Training Program (2011) reported that they initiated their research through a meeting with the local councillors at the village and subcounty level. At this meeting, the councillors recommended that women who did not have political roles should be asked to identify other women to participate in the research. At each of the meetings held to select research participants, a local council representative was present, often the vice-chair.

On the web
THE LESSONS

The report by the Foundation for Human Rights Initiative (Kabugo et al. 2011) notes that, due to the sensitivity of land issues — as well as a common African belief that all affairs regarding the home should be kept private — some of the women from whom narratives were supposed to be collected refused to share their experiences, while others would not give concrete information. These women said exposing their husbands in this way could put the men "in trouble" and might even lead to their imprisonment. They said that this would then disadvantage the woman, as, in most cases, their husbands were reportedly the sole breadwinners.

Part 5

Looking forward

In this book, we examined critical issues connected to women's rights and access to, as well as control and use of, land. It is clear that much remains to be done, and, indeed, IDRC continues to fund research in this field. This final chapter points to some areas to reflect on as we move forward.

Women's collective agency

There is minimal support for women taking charge of their demands for land rights, and efforts to address land and property issues are generally isolated and disjointed. As an organized collective, however, women present a significant political and economic force. Building alliances and partnerships and stronger women's movements will provide a more effective platform from which to advocate women's secure access to land. It will also build the capacity of women by encouraging the exchange of information about land administration systems and other practicalities that affect their land rights.

On the web
THE LESSONS

Strengthening awareness and monitoring

Addressing land injustices requires varied approaches that streamline and consolidate the numerous land laws in a given country. In addition, it is vital to establish and maintain links among research, policy, practice, and people.

Using formal legal processes is time consuming and often requires significant resources. There is an evident need to train and support a variety of roles. For example, more paralegals must be trained to understand land matters so as to interpret them and help women demand their rights. Women must also be sensitized and trained to understand land laws and policies so that they recognize when their rights are being violated and they know about the possibilities for redress. Training journalists to understand land from a woman's perspective could also help create public support for change. Knowledge exchange among developing countries and within regions could help women share their experiences and strategies for securing land entitlements.

Covering the African continent

In September 2010, when IDRC hosted an international policy symposium on "Women's Rights and Access to Land in Africa" in Nairobi, researchers from across the continent shared their findings and policy recommendations, engaged with policymakers, and promoted the development of subregional networks. Over 140 participants attended the event, coming from 17 African countries as well as international and donor organizations.

Yet, although this level of participation was impressive, the absence of representation from some parts of the continent, in particular North and Central Africa, was glaringly evident. In fact, research on gender and land is still in its formative stages.

Many subregions have hardly been covered in the work undertaken to date. A more thorough analysis is required of the existing body of research, as well as where research priorities lie in underresearched contexts.

Creating a network

The Nairobi symposium was organized, in part, to respond to the need of researchers and other actors to develop relationships with others who are active in this field and to provide a platform for sharing research methods, experiences, and findings. The next step is to determine how best to build and sustain an effective, informal network. The success of such a network will lie in its capacity to meet the needs of participants, in its ability to evolve as those needs evolve, and in its ability to establish collaborative relationships with other networks.

Policy uptake

Although individual projects have made recommendations for policy and practical uptake, participants at the policy symposium also contributed to the development of a set of general recommendations for policy and action. This document presents another opportunity to initiate discussion between policymakers and practitioners and to encourage new thinking about women and land. Much remains to be done by project partners in terms of dissemination and uptake strategies.

Areas for further research

The following are but a few of the areas that could be considered for future research on women's rights and access to land.

Gender, property rights, and violence

Early scoping studies conducted by IDRC raised concerns about how women's increased control over property may have negative repercussions in terms of male violence. They indicate that, as a result of changing responsibilities and political–economic circumstances, men feel their power diminishing and, in some cases attempt to reassert their authority through (sexually) aggressive behaviour. In cases of joint property rights, where a woman's consent may be required for lease or sale of the land, this "consent" is reportedly, at times, coerced by men asserting their control through violence. The nexus of gender, violence, and land rights is a critical area that warrants further investigation.

Children and access to land

Little research has focused on how the presence of and relationship to children affect women's access and rights to land. Research on this question has the potential to contribute to policy and planning around land claims and use at national and local levels. In some customary systems, the rights of a single or widowed woman to land can depend on whether she has children for whom she cares or, more specifically, whether she has male children.

Land grabs

New developments that complicate issues, but that also should bring renewed attention to women and land include food and fuel crises, transnational and foreign government land grabs, and large-scale infrastructure projects. Research is needed to examine the connections among these issues, women's rights, and land administration and to identify commonalities and differences in experiences across countries and regions.

Health priorities among women working and living in agro-ecosystems

Understanding the relations among women's health priorities, environmental concerns, and land access and use has implications for both women's health policy and the development of sustainable agro-ecosystems. The health burden of poverty in rural areas can include a wide diversity of environment-related conditions: malnutrition, reproductive health issues, HIV/AIDS, other infectious diseases, and chemical and physical hazards. Moreover, the impacts on women's health that flow from crop selection, soil enhancements, water, harvesting, and commercialization must become part of the discussions about food security.

A new generation of African women leaders

Finally, the importance of providing teaching and training in a variety of disciplines to a young generation of women in Africa cannot be overstated.

Research projects funded by IDRC have used several methods to ensure that young women were engaged in various aspects of the development, management, and delivery of research projects, including important work on theory and research methods. Several projects have gone further, enabling young grassroots women leaders to lead research processes both locally and nationally and showcase their work in international fora.

We hope that such methods will continue to be a part of all initiatives in this area. We believe that this approach can help create a new generation of African women researchers and leaders capable of advancing policy agendas that can result in tangible benefits for all.

On the web

THE LESSONS

Sources
and resources

This book focuses on the research that IDRC has supported on women's rights and access to land and forms an integral part of IDRC's website devoted to the subject: **www.idrc.ca/in_focus_womenandland**. The full text of the book is available online and leads the reader into a virtual web of resources, including scoping studies, outputs of all projects, videos, and conference reports.

There is a great deal of published literature about gender, land rights, and land tenure in general and this section offers a small selection of these for further study.

Bibliography

Ahikire, J. 2009. Decentralisation, women's land rights and citizenship in East Africa, workshop and policy symposium, held at the Metropole Hotel and Centre for Basic Research. Centre for Basic Research, Kampala, Uganda. Workshop report 24, 36 p.

Ahikire, J. 2011. "Cutting the coat according to the cloth": decentralisation and women's agency on land rights in Uganda. Centre for Basic Research, Kampala, Uganda. Working paper 97, 54 p.

Alinon, K. 2008. Participation à la table ronde sur l'accès des femmes à la terre en Afrique de l'Ouest : problématique et pistes de solutions au Sénégal et au Burkina Faso. International Development Research Centre, Ottawa, Canada.

Andrade, X.; Cristiano, A.; Casimiro, I.; Almeida, I. 2009. Empowering women through access to and control over land in context of gender biased green-revolution policies: action research project in Manhiça District. International Development Research Centre, Ottawa, Canada. Final report.

Banda, M.K. 2008. Securing women's access to land: linking research and action. Report on the Malawi capacity strengthening workshop. International Development Research Centre, Ottawa, Canada.

Banda, M.K.; Kamanga-Njikho, V.; Malera, G.; Mauluka, G.; Kamwano Mazinga, M.; Ndhlovu, S. 2011. Women's access to land and household bargaining power: a comparative action research project in patrilineal and matrilineal societies in Malawi. International Land Coalition, Rome, Italy. Research report 9. www.landcoalition.org/sites/default/files/publication/959/WLR_9_Malawi.pdf

Budlender, D. 2011. Researching women, land and customary law: methodology. Community Agency for Social Enquiry, Johannesburg, South Africa.

Budlender, D.; Mgweba, S.; Motsepe, K.; Williams, L. 2011. Women, land and customary law. Community Agency for Social Enquiry, Johannesburg, South Africa. cge.org.za/index.php?option=com_docman&task=doc_download&gid=195&Itemid=

Deininger, K. 2003. Land policies for growth and poverty reduction: a World Bank Policy Research Report. The World Bank, Washington, DC, and Oxford University Press, New York, USA.

Fonjong, L.; Sama Lang, I.; Fombe, L. 2009. The impact of land tenure practices on women's rights to land in anglophone Cameroon and implications on sustainable development. University of Buea, Buea, Cameroon.

Forum Mulher. 2009. Securing women's access to land: linking research and action. Report on the Mozambique capacity strengthening workshop. International Development Research Centre, Ottawa, Canada.

FVTM, RESEAU SOA, HARDI, FOFIFA, SIF. 2009. Securing women's access to land: linking research and action. Report on the Madagascar capacity strengthening workshop. International Development Research Centre, Ottawa, Canada.

Gender and Rural Development Thematic Group and the Land Policy and Administration Thematic Group of the World Bank. 2005. Gender issues and best practices in land administration projects: a synthesis report. World Bank, Washington, DC, USA. siteresources.worldbank.org/INTARD/Resources/Gender_land_full txt.pdf

GROOTS (Grassroots Organizations Operating Together in Sisterhood). 2011. Complementing the state: the contribution of the watchdog groups in protecting women's land rights in Gatundu District. International Land Coalition, Rome, Italy. Research report 4. www.landcoalition.org/sites/default/files/publication/952/WLR_4_GROOTS.pdf

Hornby, D. 2006. Report on the IDRC's Rural Poverty and
Environment Program's Gender and Tenure Study. The Southern
Africa sub-region, incorporating South Africa, Zimbabwe and
Malawi. International Development Research Centre, Ottawa,
Canada.

IDRC (International Development Research Centre). 2010.
Gendered terrain: women's rights and access to land in Africa.
Presentations from the conference, 14-16 Sept. 2010, Nairobi,
Kenya. IDRC, Ottawa, Canada.
web.idrc.ca/en/ev-158124-201-1-DO_TOPIC.html

International Land Coalition. 2011. Securing women's access to
land: linking research and action. An overview of action-research
projects in Eastern Africa. International Land Coalition, Rome,
Italy. Synthesis report 14.
www.landcoalition.org/publications/synthesis-report-action-
research-projects-women%E2%80%99s-access-land-eastern-africa

Kabugo, D.N.; Joanittah, M.; Yousouf, B.; Madiina, K.;
Foundation for Human Rights Initiative. 2011. Assessing the
implementation of the spousal consent of the Land Act 1998 and
upscaling advocacy for women's rights to access and control of
land. A case for Kayunga district, Uganda. International Land
Coalition, Rome, Italy. Research report 3.
americalatina.landcoalition.org/sites/default/files/WLR_3_FHRI.
pdf

Kanyinga, K.; Mitullah, W. 2010a. Land administration system in
Kenya and implications for women's land rights. University of
Nairobi, Nairobi, Kenya.

_____ 2010b. Women, culture and decentralized land
administration in Kenya. University of Nairobi, Nairobi, Kenya.

Kassim, S. 2011. Decentralization of land administration and women's rights in Tanzania: some experiences from Mlali village. Centre for Basic Research, Kampala, Uganda. Working paper 100.

Kenya. 1981. The law of succession act. National Council for Law Reporting, Nairobi, Kenya. www.kenyalaw.org/klr/fileadmin/pdfdownloads/Acts/LawofSucce ssionActCap160.pdf

_____ 2007. The judicature act (chapter 8). National Council for Law Reporting, Nairobi, Kenya. www.kenyalaw.org/Downloads/GreyBook/3.%20Judicature%20A ct.pdf

_____ 2009. The registered land act (chapter 300). National Council for Law Reporting, Nairobi, Kenya. www.law.co.ke/Downloads/Acts/Registered%20Land%20Act.pdf

_____ 2010. The Constitution of Kenya, 2010. National Council for Law Reporting, Nairobi, Kenya. www.kenyaembassy.com/pdfs/The%20Constitution%20of%20Ke nya.pdf

Lastarria-Cornhiel, S. 2006. Women's access and rights to land: gender relations in tenure. Issues Paper prepared for the Advisory Group Working Meeting, June 2006. International Development Research Centre, Ottawa, Canada.

Lebert, S.B.; Lebert, T. 2010. Advocacy toolbox. International Land Coalition, Rome, Italy. www.landcoalition.org/sites/default/files/Advocacy_Toolbox_ ENG.pdf

Makerere Institute for Social Research. 2010. Securing women's access to land: linking research and action. Makerere Institute of Social Research, Kampala, Uganda. Eastern Africa synthesis report.

Mazhawidza, P. 2009. Securing women's access to land: linking research and action. Report on the Zimbabwe capacity strengthening workshop. International Development Research Centre, Ottawa, Canada.

Mazhawidza, P.; Manjengwa, J. 2011. The social, political and economic transformative impact of the Fast Track Land Reform Programme on the lives of women farmers in Goromonzi and Vungu-Gweru districts of Zimbabwe. International Land Coalition, Rome, Italy. Research report 8. www.landcoalition.org/sites/default/files/publication/958/WLR_8_Zimbabwe.pdf

Meinzen-Dick, R.S.; Pradhan, R. 2002. Legal pluralism and dynamic property rights. CAPRi Working Paper No. 22. Nakirunda, M. 2011. Decentralised land administration and women's land rights in Uganda: an analysis of the legal regime, state institutional arrangements, and practice. Centre for Basic Research, Kampala, Uganda.

Panesar, J.; Fajber, L. 2006. Women's access to land: gender relations in tenure. Drawing learnings across sub-regional studies: a working document. International Development Research Centre, Ottawa, Canada.

Paradza, G. 2010. Securing women's access to land: linking research and action. Eastern Africa synthesis report 2. PLAAS (Instutite for Poverty, Land and Agrarian Studies), Bellville, South Africa.

_____ 2011a. A field not quite of her own: single women's access to land in communal areas of Zimbabwe. International Land Coalition, Rome, Italy. Working paper 11. www.landcoalition.org/sites/default/files/publication/954/WLR_11_Paradza_Zimbabwe.pdf

_____ 2011b. Differentiation of women's land tenure security in southern Africa. International Land Coalition, Rome, Italy. Working paper 12. www.landcoalition.org/sites/default/files/publication/955/WLR_ 12_Paradza_Differentiation.pdf

Procasur Research Institute. 2010. Action-oriented research and policy influence for women's access to land in Africa. The experience of Uganda and Kenya. Procasur Research Institute, Santiago de Chile, Chile, and International Land Coalition, Rome, Italy. idl-bnc.idrc.ca/dspace/bitstream/10625/45517/1/131970.pdf

Ramaroson, M.; Ramiaramanana, D.; Ravoniarisoa, L. 2011. Promoting women's access and control over land in the central highlands of Madagascar. International Land Coalition, Rome, Italy. Research report 1. www.landcoalition.org/sites/default/files/publication/1117/WLR _1_Madagascar_Web.pdf

Rao, N. 2005. Women's rights to land and assets: experience of mainstreaming gender in development projects. Economic and Political Weekly, 29 Oct.

_____ 2006. Women's access and rights to land: gender relations in tenure. A scoping study in the Indian context. International Development Research Centre, Ottawa, Canada.

Razavi, S. 2003. Agrarian change, gender and land rights. Journal of Agrarian Change, 3 (1/2): 2–32.

Ribot, J.; Peluso, N.L. 2003. A theory of access. Rural Sociology, 68(2), 153–181.

Rwanda, Republic of. 1999. Law on matrimonial regimes, liberalities, and successions. Official Gazette of Rwanda, Kigali, Rwanda. 15 Nov.
www.amategeko.net/display_rubrique.php?information_ID=678&
Parent_ID=3068178&type=public&Langue_ID=An

_____ 2004. National land policy. Ministry of Lands, Environment, Forests, Water and Mines, Kigali, Rwanda.
minirena.gov.rw/IMG/pdf/National_Land_Policy.pdf

_____ 2005. Organic Land Law. Ministry of Justice, Kigali, Rwanda.
www.amategeko.net/display_rubrique.php?information_ID=692&
Parent_ID=3068403&type=public&Langue_ID=An

Rwanda Women's Network. 2011. Experiences of women in asserting their land rights:
the case of Bugesera District, Rwanda. International Land Coalition, Rome, Italy. Research report 5.
www.landcoalition.org/sites/default/files/publication/956/WLR_
5_RWN.pdf

Rwanda Women's Network and Lawyers without Borders. 2009. Securing women's land rights: assessing gender gaps in the implementation of existing laws in Bugasera District, Eastern Province, Rwanda. International Development Research Centre, Ottawa, Canada. Inception report.

South Africa. 1996. Constitution of South Africa. Constitutional Court of South Africa, Braamfontein, South Africa.
www.constitutionalcourt.org.za/site/theconstitution/english-09.pdf

Tanzania. 1999. The village land act, 1999. Government of
Tanzania, Dar-es-Salaam, Tanzania.
www.reddtz.org/index2.php?
option=com_docman&task=doc_view&gid=12&Itemid=18

Tsikata D. 2010. Gender policies and land rights in Africa:
navigating a minefield. Presented at the IDRC symposium,
Gendered terrain: women's rights and access to land in Africa,
13–16 September 2010, Nairobi, Kenya.
web.idrc.ca/uploads/user-S/12850777521Gender_Policies_
and_Land_Rights_in_Africa-_Navigating_a_Minefield.pdf

Tsikata, D.; Golah, P., ed. 2010. Land tenure, gender, and
globalization: research and analysis from Africa, Asia and Latin
America. Zubaan, New Delhi, India, and International
Development Research Centre, Ottawa, Canada.
web.idrc.ca/en/ev-149320-201-1-DO_TOPIC.html

Uganda. 1995. Constitution of the Republic of Uganda, 1995.
Government of Uganda, Kampala, Uganda.
www.ugandaembassy.com/Constitution_of_Uganda.pdf

_____ 1998. Land Act. Government of Uganda, Kampala,
Uganda.
www.scribd.com/doc/23824390/Uganda-Land-Act-1998

_____ 2004. The land (amendment) act, 2004. Government of
Uganda, Kampala, Uganda.
www.mtti.go.ug/index.php/downloads/doc_download/376-land-
ammendment-act-2004pdf.html

_____ 2010. Land sector strategic plan, 2001–2011. Ministry of
Lands, Housing and Urban Development, Kampala, Uganda.
www.mlhud.go.ug/index.php?option=com_docman&task=doc_de
tails&gid=3&Itemid=60

Uganda Land Alliance and Uganda Media Women's Association. 2010. Women's gains from the implementation of succession law in Uganda: voices from Wakiso and Mpigi districts. International Development Research Centre, Ottawa, Canada. Final report.

Uganda Rural Development and Training Program. 2011. Voices of women's aspirations over land and land matters: the case of Kibaale district, Uganda. International Land Coalition, Rome, Italy. Research report 7. www.landcoalition.org/sites/default/files/publication/957/WLR_7_URDT.pdf

UN (United Nations). 1948. Universal declaration of human rights. United Nations, New York, NY, USA. www.un.org/en/documents/udhr/

_____ 1979. Convention on the elimination of all forms of discrimination against women. United Nations, New York, NY, USA. www2.ohchr.org/english/law/cedaw.htm

Verma, R. 2007. "Without land you are nobody": critical dimensions of women's access to land and relations in tenure in East Africa. International Development Research Centre, Ottawa, Canada. Scoping study for East Africa.

Young Widows Advancement Program. 2011. Assisting Kayole widows in gaining control to family land. International Land Coalition, Rome, Italy. Research report 10. www.landcoalition.org/sites/default/files/publication/951/WLR_10_YWAP.pdf

Partnerships

In the course of supporting this research, IDRC has collaborated with several international organizations and donor partners, which also work on land tenure issues. Readers are recommended to view material on land rights and access on their websites listed below.

Canadian International Development Agency	**www.acdi-cida.gc.ca**
Food and Agriculture Organization of the United Nations	**www.fao.org**
Ford Foundation	**www.fordfoundation.org**
Huairou Commission	**www.huairou.org**
International Fund for Agricultural Development	**www.ifad.org**
International Institute for Environment and Development	**www.iied.org**
International Land Coalition	**www.landcoalition.org**
Norwegian People's Aid	**www.npaid.org**
Swedish International Development Cooperation Agency	**www.sida.se**
United Nations Human Settlements Programme	**www.unhabitat.org**
United Nations Development Programme	**www.undp.org**
World Bank	**www.worldbank.org**

Organizations supported by IDRC

Centre for Applied Research on Rural Development, Madagascar	**www.fofifa.mg**
Centre for Basic Research, Uganda	**www.cbr-ug.org**
Community Agency for Social Enquiry, South Africa	**www.case.org.za**
Fédération des Femmes Rurales, Madagascar	
Forum Mulher, Mozambique	**www.forumulher.org.mz**
Foundation for Human Rights Initiative, Uganda	**www.fhri.or.ug**
GROOTS, Kenya	**www.groots.org**
Harmonisation des Actions pour la Réalisations d'un Développement Intégré, Madagascar	**www.hardi-madagascar.org**
Institute for Poverty, Land and Agrarian Studies, University of Western Cape, South Africa	**www.plaas.org.za**
Lawyers without Borders, Rwanda	**www.lawyerswithoutborders.org**
Makerere Institute for Social Research, Uganda	**misr.mak.ac.ug**
Reseau Syndical des Organizations Agricoles, Madagascar	
Rwanda Women's Network	**www.rwandawomennetwork.org**
Solidarité des Intervenants sur le Foncier,r Madagasca	**www.sif-mada.com**
Uganda Land Alliance	**www.ulaug.org**
Uganda Rural Development and Training Program	
University of Buea, Cameroon	**www.ubuea.net**
University of Ghana	**www.ug.edu.gh**
University of Nairobi (Institute of Development Studies and Faculty of Law), Kenya	**www.uonbi.ac.ke**

University of Zimbabwe	**www.uz.ac.zw**
Women Farmers Association, Zimbabwe	
Women's Legal Resource Centre, Malawi	
Young Widows Advancement Program, Kenya	**www.youngwidowskenya.org**